TESTIMONIALS

This book gives a great insight into what makes a chef 'tick', or what makes them even become chefs. For so long there has been a misunderstanding of why chefs can be so highly strung and challenging personalities.

If you take the time to read and think about some of the answers in this book it will give you insight and maybe even want to make you become a chef yourself.

Cooking is about a selfish pursuit of excellence and at the same time the total sacrifice of giving to others. That can be in your knowledge, your craft or your time.

We work in a temporary artistic medium that is only at its best for a short while. This creates pressure and frustration, previously misinterpreted as arrogance.

Through communication, care and understanding, thankfully we have moved on from those days and now can celebrate our excellence and complexity.

Reading through, I see that these are all successful chefs who have the grounding of good family support and a commitment to seeing it through. Both of these points are the keys to success.

They have evolved into the chefs they have become, through hard work and a never give up attitude.

For me it's simple... Cooking professionally is not a job, it's a way of life. It's exciting and a rollercoaster, but you learn about life and love along the way and that is its greatest reward.

There has never been a better time to be a chef.

~ **Michael Moore,** *Chef/Owner O Bar and Dining in Sydney. He has owned and managed numerous top restaurants both in London and Sydney.*

T0362964

This book is a must-read for anybody wanting a realistic and truthful insight into the hospitality industry. With firsthand insight from many of Australia's leaders from all walks of the industry.

~ **Liam Tomlin,** *International chef, restaurateur and author who has garnered many accolades including the much coveted 3 Hats Award and the Restaurant of the Year title. Recognized by British Airways as a member of the prestigious 'Taste Team'. Liam now lives in Cape Town SA.*

———————— ··· ————————

Congratulations Juliana, on a wonderful collection of stories from those who have served the industry on the front line. Reading through the extraordinary list of talent I am pleased to see many well-known and familiar names, many I know personally and have had the pleasure to work with and on occasion socialize with.

Many things have changed over the years and it is refreshing to see that so many chefs are now taking their own physical and mental health more seriously. They are eating better, exercising and taking time out for themselves and their families. This is fundamental in our industry where the hard work, long hours, at times harsh conditions and the elevated stress levels have claimed many relationships and sad to say even lives over the years.

As always with creative thinkers the passion levels are high and the pride in the chef whites is as strong as ever. Chefs are caring more about product and sustainability. They have respect for the food. They are conscious of food waste and maintaining the integrity of the food they produce. They are constantly pushing the envelope and coming up with new, imaginative ways of preparing and presenting food so that when the masses gather, their senses will be stimulated and the taste buds aroused. One chef commented that food is subjective and that you won't please everyone, but that won't stop them from trying.

Comradery within the brigade is akin to a dysfunctional family at times, but a family nonetheless. Floor staff and kitchen work together these days in a symbiotic relationship, each relying on the other to achieve their goals.

Their stories take me back to my early days, the friends I made then that I still have today. The opportunities to travel and the food! Wow. What other occupation would give you the opportunity to taste and eat such a vast array of produce from the freshest crispest apple to the sweetest seafood?

I would certainly recommend this book to anyone thinking of joining hospitality. It will change your life!

~ **Paul Butler,** *Food and Beverage Manager at National Press Club of Australia.*

Chefs Stories Unmasked is an essential read for anyone looking at entering into a career as a chef. The book is written well and uncovers truths of the kitchen which you would not know without industry experience. It's the next *Kitchen Confidential.*

~ **Roy McVeigh,** *Executive Chef at Restaurant Eighty Eight – The Convent, Hunter Valley.*

When I read these stories and interviews it not only takes me back to hard lessons learned in the kitchen, but in life as well. You shake your head and go "That's it." It's so true. So, when you get industry mavericks, academics, superstars and quiet achievers sharing their wisdom with those who care to listen it has to have a positive outcome.

There are serendipity moments where a visit to a place, a meeting with a mentor, a life choice shared with family have sent the chef on a career path they couldn't foresee has shaped that person and maybe industry to be forever changed. Career paths of the successful are fascinating, but it is your own path that will be challenged and rewarded at every turn on the road to success and ultimately be interesting.

A common thread these industry enthusiasts champion is the need to create time to disengage from our work. To invest time in our families and to listen to our bodies. No doubt that the hospitality industry can be tough, but we are now smart enough to realize the need to manage our lives and careers to be balanced for ourselves.

A chef is a tradesperson you expect to follow industry standards just like your electrician. They are a craft person that practices their craft demonstrating years of skill and experience. They are artisans blending personal interpretation with visual and palate balance. They are financial magicians that somehow manage all the competing interests of a catering operation. A chef is a proud and noble pursuit and these interviews demonstrate that on a very personal level.

For myself personally, I work in a workshop, it just happens to be a kitchen. I walk in and ask, "What will I build today?" After 40 years of cooking, I'm still as engaged and enthusiastic as ever because there is always something interesting to do. Hospitality is a broad family and there is a place out there for everyone. You just have to ask yourself what you want to do.

~ **Steve Baar,** *Executive chef at University House – a private club for academic staff at Melbourne University.*

CHEFS STORIES Unmasked

GLOBAL
PUBLISHING
G R O U P

Global Publishing Group
Australia • New Zealand • Singapore • America • London

CHEFS STORIES

Unmasked

A Collection of Inspirational
Stories and Lessons Learned on
their Road to Success

JULIANA FRANCES

First Edition 2019

National Library of Australia
Cataloguing-in-Publication entry:

Chefs Stories Unmasked: A Collection of Inspirational Stories and Lessons Learned on their Road to Success - Juliana Frances

1st ed.
ISBN: 9781925288865 (pbk.)

 A catalogue record for this book is available from the National Library of Australia

Published by Global Publishing Group
PO Box 517 Mt Evelyn, Victoria 3796 Australia
Email Info@GlobalPublishingGroup.com.au

Printed in China

For further information about orders:
Phone: +61 3 9739 4686 or Fax +61 3 8648 6871

This book is dedicated in appreciation for the food itself, to the growers, producers and those who prepare, cook and serve, all working together for feeding and nurturing people and the animals.

Juliana Frances

ACKNOWLEDGEMENTS

First and foremost I am profoundly grateful to everyone who contributed to the composing of *Chefs Stories Unmasked*. Each story spoke of guidance for those considering a profession in hospitality. Creative abilities can be adapted, but what is fundamental is enthusiasm, passion and commitment to why you all love cooking. That is what you bought to the table. This book would be a shadow of itself without your input.

A special thank you to each of your mentors, your team, family, and friends for providing guidance, advice, and love that have helped you at some point in varying degrees of difficulty. You are the unseen heroes.

A huge thanks to Global Publishing Group. It has been my privilege to work with Darren Stephens and his extraordinary diligent team who have brought this book as an idea to fruition. My heartfelt thanks to all of you.

Karen Winter, you were by my side helping with editing and ideas plus giving me such invaluable guidance. A big hug to you.

I relied on the support of my friends, Marinka Dunlop, Valeska Maher, Dinah Morgan, Lancia, Ida, Solana, Dede, Bert Elswyk, Kath Moody, and Gitama Day, all who generously gave of their time. Thank you also to Taryn Astill from Solotel for adding some wise words of insight.

Hopefully, my friends will understand my absence since starting this project.

To David and Wood, thank you for the care and love you have given me. You are a constant source of inspiration to so many people. Thank you for being such great sons.

And as always, I am most deeply indebted to my husband Tony, for his wise counseling, support and so very much more. You are such an amazing person.

I can now make time to finish that cup of tea!

~ Understand the power and glory
in creating and contributing.

FREE BONUS OFFER

As a thank you for purchasing this book Juliana Frances has kindly offered an additional surprise Celebrity Chef interview.

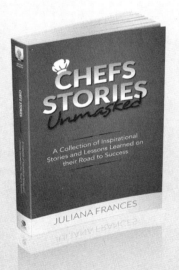

**Simply go to
www.JulianaFrances.com
to download this amazing interview.**

CONTENTS

FOREWORD

I was delighted when presented the opportunity by Juliana to write this book foreword.

A book aimed to hopefully attract, inspire or at least provoke the idea of joining the rich hospitality industry our country offers. This book shares the wonderful, unique and sometimes arduous, toilsome road to success. With every contributing story as unique as their culinary footprint.

People choose to work in hospitality for many different reasons, whether it be a deep connection to food through family childhood memories or simply left school early, fell into a kitchen and became addicted to the fast-paced, high pressure, team driven environment.

But the success of the individuals in this book aren't collectively associated by a university degree or higher education. The common ground is the drive and passion to create and please other people, whilst pursuing excellence in what they love. This is hospitality. It is one of life's greatest rewards to help create an experience that can provoke happiness, enjoyment and memories for others. I hope this book helps to encourage and excite young people into the countless career options this extended hospitality industry offers.

Troy Rhoades-Brown

Troy has a dedicated love and attention for running Muse Restaurant, which delivers a complete dining experience through a passionate, professional team gaining many accolades. He was awarded the 2005 Brett Graham Scholarship, 2014 Appetite for Excellence National Young Restaurateur and 2015 National Next Gen Chef.

INTRODUCTION

Cooking is a specialty and a decent cook is an expert.

This exciting book is written for those wishing to investigate the culinary world. It is a collection of stories from chefs and growers of fine food who share their stories with a sensitivity of emotions, supporting opportunities for those embarking on a culinary career. From hospitality to restaurant management which includes chef jobs that are no longer tied to traditional kitchens. Be it cooking on tour buses, cooking on a station in outback Australia, or fine-dine cooking on a jumbo jet serving nutritional value of foods.

This book brings attention to thinking outside the box when it comes to where or what you'll cook. Having access to some world-class food, food consciousness is starting to come into people's awareness including such things as quality, taste, and presentation. Sustainability has made a persevering responsibility to environmental principles in business tasks.

First of all, I wish to express that I am not a chef. I am a mother who loves to cook, inspired by my mother's talents in cooking. Gaining experience being a restaurant building owner and working in hospitality, I feel a need to express my thoughts on what I have seen, and experienced, and to personally expand the mindset of those working in the hospitality industry.

At the heart of each story of each person interviewed is an individual response to a basic inquiry. "For what reason do you cook?" Everybody cooks, but true cooks understand that there is a difference between why they cook in their own distinctly individual ways.

A number of critical and important issues need to be raised within the hospitality industry. We need good staff who are committed and prepared for the long periods of involvement and diligent work. It is such an aggressive industry. It can mean long hours, split shifts, cuts, burns, along with the aching back or sore feet after a busy night.

There has been a trend to get students to go on to higher tertiary training. Many who finish university may not get a job and are still required to pay back their HEC fees, resulting in levels of debt.

On the off chance that you're fresh out of education or preparing vocational change to work as a chef, this means you get the chance to work with food every day. Your colleagues most likely will become your closest friends.

Taking into account the nuts and bolts of trade school, joined with long stretches of line preparing, these are the fundamentals in becoming a great chef. It requires commitment and order. To those genuine ones who comprehend what it is they are entering into and are prepared, willing, capable and focused on a vocation, whatever the individual expenses and physical demands.

Build a reputation for your work ethic. Be fully dedicated, or you will be questioning the insight of your chosen path.

Ask yourself "Would you be able to keep up? Are you ready for service? Would you be reliable to appear at work when required, to not disappoint the team? Will you always be on time and without making excuses or blaming others?" Prepare yourself to take requests, give orders when fundamental and live with the result of those requests without dissension. This is what matters to be fully committed and dedicated.

There is the drive within to excel. Working with other imaginative gourmet specialists is extremely compensating, on the grounds that simply being around them advances your life to such an extent.

Creativity moves and feeds innovativeness. Envisioning and dreaming things in a single piece of your life creates you in your masterful undertakings. Be inventive at each twist and turn. Indeed, have frivolous thoughts. Simply appreciate each dish you cook. Be they burnt or under-cooked! Learn from each mistake, trial-and-error, and renew your respect with each flavor, and ingredient with confidence.

Focus on embracing your creativity and utilizing it as motivation. Take after and sustain each imaginative idea, for they will nourish and motivate more of you. Read lots of cookbooks for recipes and to hone concepts, techniques and skills. Remember to take time to have a laugh and a sense of humor about things.

A chef wears many hats.

With the management and business side of managing or owning a restaurant, you must have a decent comprehension of cash, product, people management and advertising. So know about how a kitchen works, chat with providers and get savvy over spending plans. Be decent and pay close attention to your staff for they will reward you. Teamwork is critical.

What is occurring behind the kitchen door?

Kitchens are loud, upsetting hot spots and some are abusive environments that cause stress. Depression is genuine and in some extraordinary cases can result in physical, mental confusion and even suicide in some cases. Kitchen life can empower workaholism, alcohol, drug and substance abuse, with gambling addictions and sometimes thwarted ambition.

How cooks and chefs manage this pressure is by a wide margin more essential than the presence of this unavoidable reality. Be responsible for the worry in your life and don't give it the upper-hand. With the help of family and friends, know they are ready and willing to listen to you. Don't suffer in silence. Talk to someone. Take time out for a power walk, eat nutritional food, work effectively under strain and keep your self-control. At any time you have the capacity, close your eyes and dream about something exciting.

You feel your most noteworthy accomplishments are when you empower others to achieve an objective. Assume responsibility on your own part. Approach your vocation with the objective of helping other people. It will effectively fabricate a network of individuals who have your back, and you will discover work fulfilment and satisfaction together.

You aren't a disappointment until the point when you quit. Realize that any individual who has made progress today has fizzled somehow yesterday. So in this way, never let overwhelm overload you. Make it your closest companion. Embrace the courage to be vulnerable.

The work involved around creating kitchen environments that are no longer that old school mentality is now about not only creating a space for chefs to be happier, also creating spaces that are nurturing, safe and inspiring for all – different races, ages and genders, etc. It's now an environment that has flexibility for working parents, cares about giving back to society, building up people's skill set as individuals – not just as cooks – and beliefs in protecting our precious earth and resources.

Being a chef implies enormous sacrifices. It tends to be a standout amongst the most fulfilling, quick paced, transient and consistently changing professions around. Each activity has its own highs and lows – yet on the off chance that functioning as a gourmet expert is your fantasy work, you'll adore it. Regardless of what the hardships, the challenges and the agonies are, there's no other life.

Regardless of what your job is within the hospitality industry, it will take you to where you want to go. Be adventurous. Satisfaction comes when living your life with purpose. If you love it, the world is your oyster. Many doors will open and you will be successful.

As you experience this book, you will find that each story has a wide range of human feelings and emotions. The ongoing theme that goes through is the basic and superseding spirit of success.

It's in moments of decision your destiny is created.
~ Darren Stephens

Andre Kropp

Employed by the Federal Group as Executive Chef observing a brigade of 70, and mentors young chefs in competition, training and education. Plus takes a personal interest in international cooking competitions. Elected National Vice President of the Australian Culinary Federation 2015-present.

ANDRE KROPP

What is your management style?

I have very much an open door policy. I lead by example, both actively and physically. I have close to 70 chefs within my brigade. Obviously, I can't create and execute every menu myself, so I employ people with my philosophy to what I put into food, as I know what they put on the menu is very similar.

Describe the relationship between the back-of-house and front-of-house operations?

Traditionally there was an anger management thing between chefs. We were all grumpy old or young chefs. We told waiters what to do and did it with our voices! Nowadays things have changed drastically.

Front-of-house staff are the salespeople who sell what we do. We have to work very closely with them and allow them to have the passion for food that we have. We want them to up-sell our menu to our guests. This relationship has to be strong and we cannot think of them as second rate staff. We have to respect what they do and they will have respect for us in turn.

Is there a secret for a successful restaurant?

The overall secret to success is delivering an excellent product that is consistent in every way. People judge you on consistency and decide whether to come back or not. Serving the same quality standards encourages people to come back. These days it is what the restaurant looks like − How it operates, how the restaurant is, and how the tables are dressed has taken a second backseat. There is a 'theatre' relationship with food. People are quite happy to eat in a rustic surrounding because the food reflects that rustic nature and there is the theatre.

What to do to stay current on the trends?

Research online and social media deliver an incredibly useful tool for us. The knowledge we have at our fingertips is huge. We can visit local growers, small suppliers and farmers to find out what they do. Seeking out seasonality is big.

Actually going out meeting friends at restaurants in other states and countries is important. This takes time and money invested back. The knowledge you gain keeps your menu current.

Describe your knowledge of food safety.

Food and work safety for me is absolutely important, especially when we are sending out two and a half thousand meals a day. The last thing we want is people coming back with alleged food poisoning. We run a food safety plan which is current and continually audited. I ensure my staff is well educated so that they understand the pros and the cons of food safety.

How do you handle stress and pressure placed within yourself and your staff?

Golf is my stress release, but it is going from a stressful environment to another. Ha ha!

Stress can overtake you and be harmful, so you have to be able to manage work and time off. Balance is essential. I am strict with myself on days off. I don't even check my emails until I return to work. This allows me to be able to spend time with my family and give 100% to my kids, my wife, family and friends outside of work. That's how I manage myself.

I believe that we all have to arrive at work with a smile and to work with a smile on our faces. I manage any issues I have on that day, or I will have the solution ready for the next day. I address problems face to face and have an open door policy.

When are you happiest at work?

All the time, as I appreciate being in the kitchen producing food. I am not unhappy sitting in meetings taking time away from my staff.

What is the best way to lead a team?

Being aware of your team is very important. When I work with people, I do the lowest job for my staff to see me doing it. I want my staff to learn how to do it. I'd rather take a step back and top and tail beans for two hours, so that other staff learn how to butcher a side of beef, for example. This gives staff the opportunity to learn, to believe in themselves, and to gain respect for what they can do.

How do you work with suppliers?

Respect is important to me and if you show your suppliers respect, they will look after you. I always tell the supplier to treat me as their guest too. If they are out of stock and I can't supply my guests, they get upset. Suppliers have to give me enough notice if something is unavailable so that I am to be able to provide a substitute which will enhance my guest's experience.

How do you wind down after busy service?

When I get home I like to walk the dog, or take my girls for a walk on the beach and spend time with them. The old days of finishing up and going to the pub and having a few beers only happens every now and then. For me to go home and spend time with my family is the way I wind down, with a nice drop of wine.

Believe in yourself as a chef, showcase yourself on the plate. What you put on the plate is representative of yourself. So if you are true to the food and respect the food, people will respect who you are.

Ash Martin

Executive chef
Homage Restaurant,
Spicers Hidden Vale,
Queensland.

ASH MARTIN

What is something that you would like other people to know about you?

Being a chef now for 16 years, it's something that I really enjoy. Yet passion about sustainability and working with farmers is probably the biggest thing that I want people to sort of understand.

Can you explain about the sustainability?

We are not fully sustainable but made a conscious decision to take a dedicated approach to ethical sustainable practices at Homage. We joined the Earth Check and Evaluate Plus Program to reduce our wastewater and electricity usage as a way of measuring our results. We grow all of our own produce in the market garden plus grow our own chickens to reduce food mileage and to verify origin and freshness, with the help of bees for pollination. So everything that we grow and cook has a story and reason behind why we are selling or cooking it. With it brings soul and feelings, especially working and dialoguing with the local farmers.

What keeps you motivated on a daily basis?

I'm not one for emails or sitting down or anything like that. The biggest motivation for me is coming to work and it's the team that's here. So we have been able to develop a really good team here with 11 chefs in the kitchen plus front-of-house staff. Surrounding yourself with good people always is a good thing, makes for good food and good times and all that sort of stuff. Definitely, the people I work with is the reason I come to work. And we're a very close team. I say that cheffing is probably the closest thing to a team sport you could possibly do without playing a sport that is.

It's just about looking after each other and you know you're only as good as your weakest link. The biggest thing is coming to work and being creative with a bunch of creative people. There's nothing else I'd rather do.

What is the best way to lead a team?

By definitely leading, not by managing. I think it's a big conscious effort. With the help of my wife, we're not bosses. We're very much a part of the team. I still sweep up the walls. I sit down with the apprentices and the other chefs to create menus. It's not just myself. Everyone has ideas, some ideas can be horrible. Having everybody engaged is probably the best way to learn and really helps with the morale.

Where do you get your creativity from?

Probably the creativity comes from a thing we do call 'beer and brains' where we have a couple of beers. We see what seasonal treasures are in the garden. You know when the mulberries are going to be ready, or the strawberries. We find the main ingredient and then just sort of grow ideas from that. I find that looking at cookbooks for photos are good, but you need to really find your own style and your own flavor. Cheffing is an art form and it's subjective. Some people love it, some people hate it. It's just trying to find your own path and your own flavors really.

What cheers you up?

The thing that really cheers me up is the guests that join our market garden tour every day. They check out our preserving room, coal pit to the smokehouses and all that sort of stuff just walking around and saying what we do on the property. Their eyes light up and they get so excited about what you do. Sometimes you can take for granted what you do at work. You might think, "Oh shit, I've got to do this today or I'll do whatever." But when you take the guests for a walk for half an hour at five o'clock you actually go back into the kitchen completely pumped with more excitement because you look at their eyes and they just go "Oh my God!" The guests drive my excitement and drive my will to keep on keep pushing.

How much do emotions play in a kitchen?

Hundred percent, hundred percent. We used to work 15 hours a day. Now it is only 8-10 hour days, and we're going for a run on our break, and eating healthy staff dinners at night time. Really if you feel good inside it brings a lot to mental health.

Mental health is a big thing in hospitality. For example, the 'RU OK?' campaign. It's no different than any industry. I think with chefs, it was always "Toughen up, deal with it" approach. A lot of people talk about it which is a really good thing. It's something that is being really focused on and looked at.

We address these issues, plus look at fitness, and have in place a policy of no alcohol abuse. We maintain an awareness around alcohol and health obligations that heavy drinking in the workplace or after work is not promoted. Most of our chefs go on a five km run on their break rather than going to sit down at the shed and punch back a couple of cigarettes. Energy promotes energy, even if you're knackered or whatever, you come back to work. You feel a lot better within yourself.

At the end of busy service, what do you do to wind down?

Laugh! We generally sit around as a team and have a knock-off beer...and we have a post-service briefing. So we'll say what worked, what didn't work before you get in your car and go home. It's a really nice way just to wind down and sort of stay on a positive note for the following day.

Food is subjective much like art. Some people will love it, some will hate it! If you're happy with what you're doing and how you are cooking, don't listen to everyone's opinion. Just stick at it and do what you think is best and it will all come together.

Billy Fox

Captain of the Australian Culinary Youth Team.
Worldchefs Young Chef Ambassador for Australia.
Co-Chair of the NSW Young Chefs Club.
National Winner of the 2018 Nestlé Golden Chef's Hat Award.

BILLY FOX

What attracted you to become a chef?

I enjoy cooking. I felt quite good at cooking as a young bloke. Yeah, I just kept going with cooking. I went to a careers Expo as a school excursion and I met the guy that ended up being my sous-chef through my apprenticeship, Marty Barmin. I did some work experience and then worked as a kitchen hand before I started my apprenticeship. I did the entirety of my apprenticeship under Peter Washbourne. He was a really good mentor for me through my apprenticeship and continues to be so. I did a couple of competitions as an apprentice which sort of led me into what I'm doing now with Worldchefs and the national team.

Can you please explain these competitions?

I am really fortunate as I get to travel quite a bit. I just got back from representing Australia in Malaysia with the Worldchefs Congress. That was an awesome experience for me to meet two thousand chefs from all over the world. Especially meeting some of the best chefs in the world for me to see what is out there on a global stage and see what was going on in that aspect.

As part of that, I am the chairman of the New South Wales Young Chefs Club. This is a network for young chefs, which is a product of Worldchefs and the Australian Culinary Federation. We work together to keep young chefs keen and motivated. We put on a whole bunch of master classes and networking events through the year for them to be involved and engaged.

What do you need help with most often?

I suppose not ignoring it, our industry can be tough at times. Mental health is a big thing within this industry. It can get tough working in such a fast-paced environment. So that is something that young chefs and chefs in general, need to be really mindful of. There is a growing support network now and chefs are becoming more aware, but they really need to keep an eye on their health.

What's the best part of being a chef?

As chefs, we like to cook for people. It's just the nature of who we are. For me personally to travel is a great aspect. In this industry with this particular skill set, it is easy to head overseas and find work. That is a really good part about what we do.

We've also really fortunate in Australia because we have access to some of the best produce in the world.

What is the most amazing dish you have created?

I like to continually create different things, without lingering on specific dishes for too long. I really like working with seafood, especially at home. Australia has such wonderful and diverse seafood and I think Aussies should be eating more of it. So I suppose I don't really have a favorite dish.

Have you any tips that you can share from your job?

Yeah, be mindful that there is a certain level of stress that comes with the kitchen. You need to chill out. At the end of the day, you need to maintain the fact that you're doing your best. The stress is something that you need to leave at the door.

How would you spend an unexpected three days paid leave?

At the moment I'd jump on a plane to Tasmania to do some of the food scenes down there. The restaurants and producers are doing incredible stuff and the produce itself is the best in the country at present.

Do you read lots of chef books or watch cooking shows?

Anthony Bourdain books are my favorite, his books are great. As for TV shows, I only watch a little bit. Again, I like Anthony Bourdain's 'Parts Unknown'. It's a good cultural immersion with food all around the world is something that I'm really interested in.

What's the comradeship like within all the chefs and with the world cooking?

Look, to be a chef and wear a chef's jacket is to become part of the family I suppose.

We all know what it's like. We all share the fact that we know what a busy service is and we know what it's like to stand in between someone's meal and a very hungry customer. So yeah, we are very supportive of each other, we're the best of friends.

Chefs are some of the best mates you will find anywhere in the world because chefs care about people. That's why they are in the industry.

Do you also get adrenaline from cooking?

Yeah, look absolutely you get adrenaline, especially the service. Food prepping is not so exciting. But running a good solid service is a great feeling if you're on par. You turn around and see ten chefs going hammer and tongs to get everything done together. It's like one of the best feelings in the world. It's like one solid big team with one goal, despite where anyone comes from, their backgrounds or whatever their position. It's an incredible feeling.

Hard work beats talent when talent doesn't work hard.
~ **Tim Notke**

Brad Adams

Image Courtesy of Russell Ord

A commercial abalone diver researched and developed innovative artificial reefs for commercial aquaculture ocean farming of abalone.

BRAD ADAMS

What are your greatest professional strengths?

I am a reasonable organizer so I'm very persistent. I believe I'm also very thorough and have a real passion for this business. I find that people who are passionate about what they do, always find a way generally to succeed.

What did you do to overcome any personal defeats?

First of all, you feel sorry for yourself. Then you think, well what have I learned from this? What can I do better next time? So you know obviously life is full of ups and downs and I think when you had your downs you need to take stock and learn what you could do better next time. So it's just as important as having success as having failures.

What keeps you motivated on a daily basis?

Well, I love my job. I love what I'm doing and get really excited to be doing something so unique and having a great team around me. I get a lot of support from our board, investors and staff that we have. So you know we've developed a really good team here. Yeah, that keeps me motivated and includes every day.

What do you consider to be your weaknesses if any?

Weaknesses! I have plenty of weaknesses, but I can get a bit pushy at times when I want things done. Sometimes I go like a bull at a gate. I think I should reflect more at times rather than be so gung-ho at times. And I get told!!

What are some of the common mistakes people make achieving success?

Well sometimes perhaps people overestimate their capabilities that can result in not achieving the optimum outcome. But you have to shoot for the sky. Through not being thorough enough, and following up on specific details; even sometimes it pays to know your legal details. All of which can have you come undone, because you started becoming focused on getting something happening, without noticing the small oversights that can actually escalate later on.

How do you inspire others?

By example, being motivated, wanting to go the extra mile and be enthused is the best way.

Who has inspired you the most in the past?

I have had many mentors in the past that I respect and have had the opportunity and ability to call them and have discussions with them. Also some of my peers with other people in the business that I know, I have been able to talk to them about where we're going. So I have been able to develop a reasonable support network around me to be able to discuss things and a good rapport with them as well.

What's your vision for the future?

My vision for the future is to continue growing the business and developing new businesses elsewhere in our field and becoming a vertically integrated seafood company.

Do it now.

Charles Carroll

CEC, AAC, HOG

Executive Chef, River Oaks Country Club, USA.
Past President of The World Association of Chefs Society.
Eight times Culinary Olympian.
Award Winning author.
A host of 'The Recipe Podcast: Celebrities Secrets to a
Successful Life.'

CHARLES CARROLL
CEC, AAC, HOG

What is something you would like other people to know about you?

I have been blessed to enjoy many experiences and opportunities, but all of them came with tons of hard work. We have a great culinary program at River Oaks Country Club in Houston Texas. I enjoy watching young culinarians grow into positions of leadership.

I have designed, raised hundreds of thousands of dollars and produced shows for our troops in Afghanistan. We gave away tons of gifts and fed our troops a home cooked meal while entertaining them with seven Vegas-style shows. I have been a part of eight different Culinary Olympic Teams. I have met and visited with four United States Presidents, award-winning author of three books. Most importantly, being the father of two amazing girls who continue to make me proud every day.

What work ethics are the most important to you?

For myself personally, it's dedication, commitment, follow-through, and possessing the will to 'want to be great' and not just wish to be great. I am frustrated with today's environment with the people not following through. I will have ten people apply for a job, six will set an appointment to come in and only three will show up. I have chalked it up to the internet, smartphones and today's way of communicating. Everybody can conduct business on their phone, just 'swipe' or 'agree' and later weigh their options. It is a bad way of doing business. If you're a young professional out there, just know that eventually, this way of doing business will not serve you well.

Be who you say you're going to be!

Do what you say you're going to do!

Commit 120% to what you say you're going to commit to!

What procedures enhance your employee's performance?

I am so passionate about this I have written two books on it!

Leadership Lessons from a Chef, finding time to be great

Tasting Success, your guide to becoming a chef

There are too many answers to this, but I am a firm believer of 'environment'. You build it and "They will come kind of thing." I do my best to be sure the employees have a fantastic environment to work in. You can achieve that with hundreds of different ways from lighting, to attitude, to a family meal. The environment is everything and that is or should be controlled by the boss, or the Executive Chef. "How the Chef goes... so goes the ship." Recognition programs, incentive programs, one-on-one meetings to discuss one's future, employee parties, leadership meetings and so on.

What does it take to be a leader in the hospitality industry?

I don't think it is getting any easier. The older generation has to try and understand the way today's generation thinks, or get out of the way. I have been thinking hard on this the past few months. Am I going to be a stubborn chef and demand that the younger generation learns as I have learned, demand that all young people work 60-80 hours a week, keep your mouth shut and do everything the chefs say because that is the way I had to do it? In my opinion, this does not work and I go back to the smartphones, the internet and social media. We have to jump on this train if we are going to stay current and find ways to 'create an awesome environment' that is better conducive to young people. So my long-winded answer is 'patience'. A great leader has to be patient and want to stay current with today's technology and be willing to find new ways to connect and build your team.

Can you share your secret recipe for success?

Again, I have been blessed to do some amazing things, none of which came because of luck. My third book is 'The Recipe: a story of loss, love and the ingredients of greatness'. We hope to start shooting the movie next year. I am working on a TV documentary series. I have a very successful podcast called, 'The Recipe Podcast, Celebrities Secrets to a Successful Life'. All of these current projects come with a ton of hard work, blood, sweat and tears. It comes from never giving up and when one idea did not work or did not catch on, it bumped me over to another path and then another and if you stick with it long enough, you will achieve your goal. It may look slightly different from the original dream, but you will achieve it if you never give up!!! The secret here is... you have to be ok with the journey! Be ok with getting bumped around. Just because something did not work out doesn't necessarily mean you failed. You're now smarter than you were and know what doesn't work…hence you got bumped over a notch or two and now on a better path to your goal. Be ok with the journey.

Do you have a sense of humor?

Shit yah…didn't you just read the last paragraph…☺

Dare to dream

Have the courage to chase your dreams

Be ok with the journey

Chris Wheelhouse

National Accounts Manager for Robins Food Industries and a gifted gourmet chef with profound information about Indigenous food.

CHRIS WHEELHOUSE

Can you please share some background to how you got started into cheffing?

I started during a recession we had to have. The only form of employment I could get was actually in hospitality. I was bought up not to accept unemployment benefits, so I went doorknocking till I could get a job.

Why do you put on your chef's apron?

You spend a lot of years in mastering your cooking skills and food knowledge. You wear it with a sense of pride, it is part of who you are and part of your journey.

What is the most challenging part of your job?

Breaking down the barriers of people's perception of Australia's native foods is challenging. They have been used for centuries, but often ignored or overlooked by mainstream Australia, but now definitely accepted as far as chefs go. It's an industry that's got its challenges and to educate people to use them and to use them with confidence like they would use any other traditional European food. It's not an easy thing to do or to balance.

What's your most loved sustenance of Australian bush food?

It just depends on what you're cooking. I think probably one of my most fascinated fruits is the bush tomato in its raw form; a desert species that has never been cultivated. Along with Aspen berries, desert limes, finger limes, riberries, lemon myrtle, the list goes on…they have unique flavor profiles. People have a perception of what something would taste like, but often it's actually completely different as to how it actually does taste and they can often go sweet or savory. They're fascinating plants.

Do you like to have things carefully planned or do you prefer to go along with the flow?

Sometimes you don't get a choice. Planning is obviously important, but sometimes you get a curveball and you just have to run with it. You don't get options. You just have to deal with it.

What's your secret talent?

I don't think I've got a particular skill. I was told to not be honed in to be a particular specialist, like somebody who might work just on stocks and sauces or soups, but rather somebody who has actually got a broad industry knowledge.

What do you need help with most often?

I think everybody needs a mentor and to embrace them. From a business sense, it's always fluid and you should really be open to criticism. The quality you may not necessarily at first agree with. Often it's from a third eye and it's actually often the truth.

What is your best business advice you've ever been given?

Never go into doing business with friends. Keep personal relationships and finance completely separate.

Have you any tips that you can share from your job?

Listen. That's probably one of the biggest tips that I can give is to actually listen to people. Often people are so busy telling other people what they want to hear that they actually forget to hear what somebody else is trying to tell them. So I would say listen.

What is the most amazing place in nature you've been to?

To sit in the forest, listen to the birds, smell the trees. It doesn't matter whether it's the beach or watching the fog roll in the bay, sitting amongst an eclipse or sitting out in the desert. Once you're outdoors just embrace it for what it is.

Would you mind sharing the longest rabbit hole you've been down?

I actually did open up a cafe for a short period of time that felt like a lifetime. And it was just a combination of many different factors that come into play, some completely outside of my control.

Having to learn on the run; understanding the complexities of signing the lease without the luxury of just getting out and walking away. Knowing when the business isn't functioning, to stop over-capitalizing or when to walk away and close the door. Be honest and ask yourself are you actually just bumbling along? Or, is it a properly functioning business that is paying its staff's full entitlement?

What are your strengths?

Being tenacious because it can be your strength, but it can also be your biggest downfall if you don't know when to pull the plug. Each circumstance is different. You know when it feels wrong within your stomach, its run its race, you know within yourself.

And having an 'off' day?

You know, it's sure as the sun gets up every morning and then the grass is green. If you think it's greener on the other side of the fence, more often it's not. Because as soon as you think it is, you sure know that the sun is going to be around the corner and brown off. So you just think of those who are less fortunate. Remember what you actually do have, not what you don't have. Know what you have as opposed to what you don't have. And then you realize you are having a good day because so many people just don't get the opportunity to wake up.

If you had a magic wand, what would it look like?

Not one for the magic that doesn't last. A bit like living in a pinball machine. You never know when someone's going to pull that spring and shoot you. Often you're going to run into something else and be knocked from one side to the other. That's just part of the journey of life.

Have you put any plans for the future?

I think you have got to plan for the future. But also be prepared that while the best-laid plans you can put in place, know they are guarded by external forces. So you've got to be prepared to take a step to the side.

*Dance like no one's watching and seeing
what I want in here.*

Cynthia Louise

Plant-based Whole Food Master Chef and creator of vegetarian & dairy-free 'Online Cooking Classes.'

CYNTHIA LOUISE

How did you get started with whole food cooking?

I grew up in Papua New Guinea, where I didn't have access to the food trends or products on supermarket shelves. My natural way of eating was from the environment around me.

I started my career working in one of Australia's leading health retreats and I came up the ranks quickly. I surrounded myself with whole foods, without processing and made everything from scratch. We used minimal frying and heat, without even browning things and good quality oils, vinegar, and sweeteners from nature.

My foundation was already there from the beginning and my career led me to the wellness industry.

What do you love about food?

I love eating food and I love training people to facilitate creativity in the kitchen.

I still have memories of my grandmother making brown bread. Every time I smell bread out of the oven, it reminds me of my grandmother.

Food sparks an interest in people. They ask "Why do you eat and cook this way?" or "Aren't you going without?" when I facilitate a chef or a mom at home. It sparks their interest and something happens to them. They acknowledge nature and start eating things from nature and feel better in their body. It's a ricochet effect.

Food brings the ultimate flow within the body. We have a great body system with amazing organs. When we eat this whole food from nature, our body knows exactly how to process it, especially for children. Food brings health and happiness and it brings us back to nature.

How does a positive attitude contribute to what you do?

We are either positive or negative. It's not predictable; it's just not how we are. It's listening to both sides that are important.

I cook because I want to cook. When I have a negative attitude I don't cook, as this makes a big impact on the outcome of the dish. I cook when I am in a happy mood.

I cook for my husband, I cook three times a day when at home. I don't have anyone cooking for me, but me. I don't get sick of cooking. But I do acknowledge when I'm a little bit irritable or getting my period or pissed off or whatever, I don't cook.

Who inspires you the most?

Jamie Oliver inspires me. He's inspired me to be loud and proud with food.

Local cultures around the world inspire me. In Indonesia and Papua New Guinea, there are so many different tribes and different ways of cooking. Other cultures that inspire me include Africa, South Africa, Australian culture and American culture.

Grandmothers to great-grandmother's cultures around the world inspire me. They are the traditional healers of our world and they use whole food. They don't use MSG, powdered mixes, milk or a lot of meat. If you ask people in Papua New Guinea or Indonesia what their grandmothers ate, it was really amazing. Those cultures really inspire me to step back into creating food in its natural state.

What do you hope to inspire in others?

I really love to inspire people especially mothers with kids, as they don't really understand the value of food. I inspire parents, in particular, those with cancer and diabetes, to really look at food in its whole form.

I ask mothers to read the packets when they are buying their children something and to identify with the numbers on the packets, what those numbers mean and what happens to the human body when you eat them. Science tells us that it's vital that we don't eat that way. We are dying early as human beings and it shouldn't be this way.

I inspire people to look at everything they purchase and to see if it is in its whole form, and to ask what they can do to get food in its whole form.

What's the most challenging part of being a chef?

I am a bit of a control freak. I don't like it and it's challenging for me to let go.

I create a dish and submit it to the chefs I'm training. Then I have to walk out of the kitchen, making sure they're making the same thing. This is the hardest thing for me to control. I have to let go and allow others to put their energy into each dish and to take that dish to a better place.

My job is to teach chefs to be better than me. If I can do that, I won't be so controlling and the food will be amazing.

Where do you get your inspiration from?

From nature, living a life of mindfulness being present all the time. I can build a menu in five minutes and create dishes in a day. I look around to see what's around me and I put that onto a plate or use a plate of wood.

What's the most amazing place you have been in nature?

Everywhere! There is not any one place. There is nature everywhere so it depends where you place your attention. I walk down the busiest street in America or Australia. It's amazing and I feel very comfortable and I can walk in the bush and feel very comfortable.

Can you tell me a motivational quote that you live by?

I facilitate cooking in the most humble kitchens around the world. I bring to light the internal not external. I believe when women look in the mirror, they look at themselves on the outside, not understand what is happening on the inside. I am facilitating people in the world to actually be able to do understand what is happening on the inside. This is a humbling experience.

Dan Hunter

Image Courtesy of Colin Page

Dan Hunter was named the Australian Financial Review's Top Chef 2016 and 2017; the Age Good Food Guide's Chef of The Year 2012 and 2016; and Australian Gourmet Traveller Magazine's Chef of the Year 2016. Brae Restaurant joined the culinary elite in the World's 50 best restaurant rankings.

DAN HUNTER

Can you please share how you got into cooking?

I spent my late teens early '20s hanging out with friends and working odd jobs. Then I got a job as a kitchen hand washing dishes at a pub in Melbourne.

I hadn't worked with food and I enjoyed being in the kitchen. Most of the time people were being themselves and there was comradery between the people working in the kitchen and the floor.

There was a lot of repetition and teamwork. I could see similarities in team sports I had played in the past. So I decided to pursue cooking, rather than washing dishes.

What would you like people to know about your restaurant?

Brae Restaurant is certainly known internationally.

The experience people in our dining room with the food they consume and the hospitality that they receive from our team is what we are known for. My wife and I talk about this and communicate it with the staff regularly.

We have a strong commitment to transforming our property to be totally sustainable. The hospitality business has been at the forefront of changing this culture.

We are introducing philosophies and viewpoints for our staff, shaping a generation of cooks in front-of-house training with a better understanding of their working environment and being less wasteful.

How does a positive attitude contribute to what do you do?

Today chefs are put on pedestals. It is not a competition to identify whose cool, who's hot, or who's the best. It's about relaxing in what you do.

We run on a tightrope all the time to make sure when people review us; when guests write about us on a blog or share us on Instagram.

You see the restaurant and our meals flashed across thousands, or tens of thousands, or hundreds of thousands of followers on social media. The positivity can be fun and pleasurable rather than critical.

What are your greatest professional strengths?

I have an eye for detail and I seem to be quite grounded. I am a good motivator and I am good at communicating my values with those in the business and the family we have established.

Those who come to Brae Restaurant recognize the restaurant as being made up of many details that become a great experience. I make sure that things are done a certain way. Success is what we do.

I think certainly having the ability setting standard for our business. These are what we achieve in whatever aspect of the business we are looking at. We make sure that we follow through and are very comfortable with each decision based on that standard completely.

What did you do to overcome defeat?

When we work with achieving certain standards every day, we are constantly evolving and we are constantly improving what we do. This means we are constantly being defeated in that sense.

We cannot control personalities, nor can we control the flow of service or every single element of cooking. This spread throughout the entire team, recognizing there are defeats. This is a by-product of achieving which allows us to get on with it and to not get so caught up in negativity.

What keeps you motivated on a daily basis?

Simple things like my daughter and my wife. And there is the commitment to our team.

Motivation is a personality trait common to people who work the way we do. You are just motivated. Not necessarily by your business, money, success or fame.

You know that generally, you have an innate motivated streak in you. You get up, you go to work and you get on with it. There's an energy level I have that is very productive.

There are times when I'm quite flat and at times, I creatively have more ideas. I wish I had more time to follow through with those ideas.

I think the most interesting thing is the amazing customer reactions and customers' responses to a truly memorable experience.

How do you dream your recipes up?

They are constantly being dreamt.

We maintain a visual perspective and concentrate on who we are; what tools we have; what region we represent; and who we are creatively. The challenge is to be creative with fewer ingredients.

I live in a beautiful part of the world. My creativity comes from life experiences and my interaction with the world.

I carry my notebook and write down my thoughts. Some are ridiculously good ideas. I wouldn't say that my creative tendencies come from in the kitchen, as often it is a very mechanical place of preparation and service.

So tell me what are some of the common mistakes people make achieving success?

Succeeding before they are ready and not retaining humility on their path.

I have no issue with sharing with the staff that I don't think our food is the most creative in the world. And I don't think that what we do is the best in the world either.

What we do is definitely us and something that we are proud of.

What's the best piece of business advice that you've been given?

Maintain good relationships, not just your customers, but with your suppliers. If you want to have a decent business, pay your suppliers on time.

What's your vision for the future?

To remain at the forefront and to be a culinary identity for Australian cuisine globally.

For the property to develop, after planting fruit trees and creating a really nice space and to become what it is designed to be.

Quality of life is important whilst providing a quality where people benefit.

People don't care how much you know until they know how much you care. ~ **Teddy Roosevelt**

Diana Scott

Pet Industry Association of Australia Supplier/Manufacturer of Excellence Award for 2017.

DIANA SCOTT

How did you get into preparing commercial pet food?

I have been feeding my family free-range organic food, being a strong advocate against factory farming.

I happened to look on the back of a dog food packet at the ingredients and was astounded. This doesn't sound nourishing. I didn't even know what a lot of the ingredients were. So I contacted an animal nutritionist and asked: "What should I be feeding my dogs?" She replied, "Raw food is the biologically appropriate diet for a dog." I asked her for a list of ingredients which she gave me. The ingredients made perfect sense.

So I got these ingredients and chopped them up in portions. This was hard work.

I went online to find a more convenient alternative which was free-range, organic and ethical. I couldn't find it! I told the animal nutritionist and she said "This is the problem most people face. So why don't you find a way?"

Then I discovered freeze-drying. This is a unique process in its own right. So I decided to make a 100% ethically sourced, freeze-dried pet food.

Tell me about the challenges you face and how you deal with them?

I suppose the first challenge I faced was in understanding how many free-range farmers there are in Australia, where to source produce and whether they would participate in this, given that I was going to use this produce for pet food. The farmers had to make a mental shift with my needs.

The way I got around this, came from the farmers themselves. There are cuts of meat from their animals that they will have a good market for in terms of restaurants and consumers, with parts they trim off that go to waste.

I said I would pay a reasonable price for them. So I actually created a market for what a farmer produces, but don't necessarily have a market for.

This is the same for organic fruit and vegetables. When you buy organic fruit and vegetables, you might expect to get some that are bent or dirty- as that's part of the organic experience.

So I go to the organic fruit and vegetable people and say, "Rather than destroying those crops, I will buy those crops from you that you can't sell."

My first challenge was to have them come on board. Would they be willing to sell me a fabulous product with me turning it into pet food? They were just as enthusiastic as I was.

My other challenge was manufacturing. I spent time talking to people and listened to the farmers. I asked them how to find a suitable manufacturing facility. People were only too happy to help me get to the next stage.

The other challenge then, was that my quantities were small. I went to a manufacturing facility and said I want to produce 1000 kilos and they laughed at me. This is because they're producing hundreds of thousands of kilos.

So I used all of my sales skills to convince them that my business would grow. I said, "I might be small to start with, I can see where this is going to go, and could you help me get there?"

I used my marketing abilities and was able to demonstrate through the use of charts and forecasting where I thought my business would go to sell the idea to them. So I was able to get these people to work with me.

In terms of manufacturing, as soon as you say pet food the manufacturers think you're talking about poor quality ingredients. This is traditionally what is used in pet food. I state that I am using top quality food and the highest quality ingredients. This is a hurdle that I had to get across.

For a small business, I have grown very quickly. I need the cash flow to buy stock. Also, sourcing investors have helped fund my rapid growth.

How do you motivate yourself to keep going?

I have a strong vision that I believe in.

In fact, as I am speaking to you I have sayings on the wall saying "End factory farming." So I'm constantly reminded just how much has been invested in this business. It would be hard to walk away now.

If I have a bad day (and I've had some let me tell you!). I get an email with a picture of a little Pomeranian, Labrador, or a Cavoodle who is shiny and happy and smiling; their owners telling me this food has changed their lives. That is an extraordinary motivator.

Can you tell me some of your professional strengths?

My background is in marketing and advertising. So I understand business development and understand intrinsically what I need to do to develop a product to market. I didn't understand manufacturing, but I did understand business and that helped me to understand the process.

When I wrote a business plan five years ago, I went from an idea to proof of concept. My strength was in understanding that I needed to do that rather than to just go hell for leather into a market that I didn't know if it exists. Having the capacity to understand that and then to be able to think outside of the square. My whole marketing strategy is based on a disruptive strategy and my ability to think differently, to use logic, but also to use creativity.

What's your vision for the future?

My vision is for the whole company to end factory farming. So it's not to create the greatest dog food or pet food on the planet. It's about making enough money so that we can start working with joint venture partners to educate people on setting up their own free-range farming.

When you consider the unconditional love, joy and companionship that your animals give to you, the very least you can do in return, is to feed them properly.

Glenn Austin

Global Hospitality Consultant and Associates, Honorary Life Member WACS 2014, Australia Culinary Federation National Life Member 2005, World Board of Chefs, Continental Director for the Pacific Rim 2010-2014 and International judge.

GLENN AUSTIN

What is your key to success?

Look at where you came from and don't forget it. Networking to build your business and work smart. Position yourself in the right place, doing the right work and do it properly.

What does your typical day look like?

In my early career, I woke up, smoked cigarettes, drank coffee and went to work 14 hours a day, pretty much every day. In the senior part of my career doing consulting for the past 18 years, I have the privilege of living on the beach. Now I walk on the beach, have a coffee and set up my day. I am currently working on projects in Panama, China and Australia. My work varies depending on what stage I am at with each project.

What is the most challenging part of your job?

As a consultant, cash flow is the greatest challenge. Building solid clients that continually pay is better than looking for one-off projects. I offer my clients a minimum of a two-year contract.

Describe your management style.

Passionate and I wear my heart on my sleeve. If something is wrong, you deal with it. These days I do more listening. If you listen to what's wrong and you listen to the people that you're working around, then you understand what's bothering them and resolve it. It's not about managing people; it's about what's going on.

Tell me about a difficult situation and how you handled it.

I reacted poorly and emotionally to the situation rather than thinking about it and practicing what I preach. I got angry and closed my mind. I quit some big jobs because of this. I am an awkward person when it comes to managing a team and I am slowly resolving this.

How are you raising professional culinary standards?

Any time I am in a position to influence those around me I revert back to my initial training and share that with others, depending on the situation I am in. I bring to the table all relevant information and styles that I have gathered in recent times that may help.

Communication skills are paramount. You have to understand your limitations. Most people write menus that are difficult to produce effectively. To raise the culinary standard, you have to write the menu based on what your business requires. Then when business flows, raise your standards. Then when you are busy, the menu will cope.

People make bad decisions under pressure because they have not written a menu capable of existing within the parameters. For instance, you use a packet of gravy mix which you mix with water, but that water needs to be boiled, then measured and even whisked to activate the thickness. But you're so damn busy that you don't have time to produce it properly. You have to understand all your limitations.

How much do qualifications matter?

Qualifications matter because they give you a sound advantage in this trade. Without basic broad level training, how do you know how to make a reduction or to do a fusion? If you don't understand the basics of classical cookery, you weren't properly trained. You need to know how to blend and fuse it with the cuisine you are doing. Rather than ending up with a fusion, you end up with confusion!

If you don't understand the basics, you won't know how to write a balanced menu. You have to study food costs and know how acids and oils react. These are what you learn in your apprenticeship that helps you throughout your career.

I know many people who have never done any formal training, who are brilliant cooks but don't understand the running of a kitchen. Nor do they understand how to formalize food costs, or how to write a specification on anything. These are basic things you learn going through your apprenticeship that is always something to fall back on.

Basic training is critical, but will it stop you from being in the industry, no? Can you learn those things as you grow older, yes you can? The problem is most of us get stuck. Once you get into a position you are happy and comfortable with, you will tend to not follow up with that extra training that you missed when you were younger.

How do you stay current with new trends as a consultant?

I have to be involved and learn as many things as I can. Do I need to understand the most modern dessert and how to do it, perhaps not? Do I need to understand there's a different type of sweetener, or if there is a different type to ingredient out there and how it may be used in a cafe or in manufacturing? To do that I look, learn, read and watch every cooking show on TV I can.

At some point, you will become inspired to travel around the world. I regularly go to markets where I see real food. I see what people are doing on the streets and then translate it into restaurant quality. Quite often some of these products need to be manufactured, so I go back to the basics and learn how to follow it through.

How do you advise your clients with their pricing benchmarks?

I set up a good marketing plan to see where they position themselves. Then I advise, write and construct what is required for them to meet the market. Then chefs follow the plan that has been put in place.

We all have a position within a business whether we are a cleaner, a gardener, a chef or a waiter. We all have a role to perform. That role is to follow the plan of the general manager or the marketing manager for that business. We all use our skills to play our part.

How do you handle stress and pressure?

Stress is when things are getting on top of you when you feel as though you are losing control. Pressure is when you have a lot of things on your plate, and you need to be well organized.

How do I handle them – probably both poorly! When I feel stressed, it is generally because I'm under pressure. So I think about why I am under pressure and what's bothering me. Then I deal with it in a logical format. Here is what I can do, here is what I cannot do and here is what is critical. Critical comes first and then work my way down the list.

Describe the relationship between the back-of-house and front-of-house staff operations.

These are both critical positions. You could be the best technician in the world, but if you're not out the front selling it means nothing. People who sell and present your food are as critical as the people who make it. They are a key factor for they show the customer that your staff is both proficient as well as friendly. As soon as the back-of-house staff realizes how important the front-of-house staff is and vice versa, the better off everyone is. They are both as equally important as each other.

What was the longest rabbit hole you have been down?

I had a full-time position as the General Manager of Disability Services in Northern Victoria. My role was to build a business for them that had a sustainable income. The CEO acknowledged that he could not rely on Government funding.

One of these businesses was a vegetable processing business with a number of people with disabilities initially harvesting 200 kilos of field vegetables a week. I took production to 90-120 ton a week. It was the most stressful, pressurized job I ever had and I swore that I would never go through vegetable processing again. I was so happy when they finally sold the business. It was a shocker and it kept me awake at night.

Now I have a client doing vegetable processing and I agreed to come on-board and reposition their business. I told him that exact story and we had a good laugh about it. At least I don't own the business and he has the money to have proper machinery built. Whereas, when I was with Human Services they had no budget and I had to beg, borrow and steal to get machinery from schoolmates!!

At all costs, we must respect and take care of our farmers. Without them, we would not have the food that enables us to cook and live. To live to eat is better than eating to live — although these are both intimately linked. When you have total respect for food, it, in turn, will respect your body. If you don't love being around fire, steel, and food, then you should go and find another job. Cooking gets into your blood and it becomes your life.

Henry Terry

Manage truffle farm and owner of Tasmanian Truffles Pty Ltd.
Finalist in MKR 2018.

HENRY TERRY

So Henry, what was it like growing up on a truffle farm?

Really, really good. I had a lucky upbringing, amazing parents and an amazing extended family, growing up on a truffle farm in Tasmania.

I have fond memories of my childhood. I absolutely love going truffle hunting because it's so exciting. It's like looking for buried treasure. I remember the first truffle trees my parents planted. They were the first ones in Australia to grow French black truffles.

I was there with the dogs that are specifically bred to sniff the truffles when it came to harvesting time. They come once or twice a week. I faked a stomach ache to get to get out of school to go hunting truffles. Being there for the first truffle hunt was really exciting. It has been such a big part of life for the whole family ever since; such an incredible journey. The truffle industry has changed dramatically since then. Our lives have changed and we just love what we do.

What's your vision for the future?

I never expected to be where I am now. We have gone from selling fresh truffles to selling the products that we make in the kitchen. This has added value to our business and created a new path. It has been amazing.

It's not something I saw coming as I wanted to be a professional cricketer. I just fell into this. I used to go to the markets in Hobart on Saturday mornings before I played cricket.

I had a lot of support with the help of my family when we first started creating products from the truffles. Customers told us what they wanted and a simple matter of what people were telling us. We listened to the market and to new ideas and pathways of marketing our products.

Now I go with the flow as opportunities present themselves. The world provides all you need. You just have to run with it as best you can.

In terms of the future, I have plans for the business and plans for myself which are more immediate.

What attracted you to become involved in cooking?

Growing up on a farm in Tasmania where you've got the best food in the world.

My family grew up eating and drinking everything that was homegrown. Granny milked the cow every morning. This culture is still present down here in Tasmania in places. I have a real love for good quality food and being on a farm. I grew up with an appreciation for this.

What's the biggest thing you've learned recently?

From starting off with a market stall led me to the cooking program on television with my sister. It was a massive learning experience. I learned a lot of culinary skills and it gave us so much.

What's your favorite part of growing truffles and cooking?

My number one favorite thing is a good truffle ice-cream.

Being able to come back to the family business and create something of value, using what I've learned along the way.

It's satisfying seeing a little bit of success. The favorite part of it for me is the growth from the truffles. I've made a lot of mistakes, but it has given me a better business sense. I have become more knowledgeable. The truffles have given me a way to grow more than anything else I could have imagined.

Would you like to share what your biggest mistake has been?

I've made some financial mistakes. It wasn't a big mistake, but it felt like a ripper at the time for me personally. People liked our products and wanted to order them online and have them home delivered.

Mum and dad didn't have online knowledge skills. So I got this company to build this website that cost a lot of money. It taught me that advice is very important, but the experience of doing the wrong thing helps you learn in a way that research cannot do.

A lot of the things you muck up at the time, you can achieve your goals from that learning experience.

You can read all the books you want, and it is good to find as much information as you can. For example, if you want to learn to swim you can read all the perfect techniques and knowledge, but really not learn till you get into the pool to swim. The experience of actually 'doing' makes you better and pushes you forward.

Is there something that you would like other people to know about you?

Being on TV made me feel like everyone knows everything about me! I'm pretty private. I love having a healthy lifestyle. I have a reasonably small circle of friends and family and I love what I do with the truffles. I'm pretty simple and I like to keep fit, try and keep it simple and love to surf, fish, run and be active.

What does nature teach you?

Spending time away from home last year gave me even more of appreciation of where I live, of having space, wildlife and nature around me.

I like the smell of truffles. I absolutely love their smell. I'm still amongst trees. If I'm in amongst nature I feel a lot more at home and feel very comfortable. It just feels natural and it feels right.

If you're stuck on an island like Tom Hanks what would you like to take?

A cricket ball. Ideally, I would take someone else to chat to. You would have to take some sort of food I reckon. Can you take just like a lifetime supply of eggs?

Juliana: I think that I would take a packet of seeds.

That's clever? Why didn't I think of chickens! A packet of seeds would be very sensible to be the go for sure; to have a varied diet to enjoy.

The two most important days in your life are the day you are born and the day you find out why. ~ **Mark Twain**

Hugh Wheeler

CEO of Wheeler's Oyster Farm & Seafood Restaurant.

HUGH WHEELER

How did you get started selling oysters?

We got into cooking oysters because we were receiving little to no return on our investment. We had to add value to our products or make them available for restaurants and clubs.

We created a shop where we retailed our products. People asked us if they could sit down and eat oysters. We provided seating in our shop and people came to eat them. Then they asked if they could have prawns, so we gave them prawns and a salad. Then they asked for fish and chips.

It was from the demand that we got into cooking seafood. We recognized this demand and built a 120 seat restaurant. We are successful because we took what unfolded and changed the way we did things. We had to survive through difficult times.

How does a positive attitude contribute to each day?

It's all about a positive attitude. To begin with, it was a relentless determination not to fail and not to give up. We had to find success in the worst possible scenario. I had to show the strength of character to get out of bed and go to work every day, no matter what. A positive attitude is in believing there is a solution.

What are your greatest professional strengths?

I am good at analyzing numbers and looking at future projections. I see the scenario and how it is likely to unfold. I am able to develop strategies based on this and make reasonably decent decisions.

I have a good ability to communicate with people and I am a good judge of character. I seek out people to employ to assist me to achieve my goals. I have been selective about the people I choose and I have mostly made good choices.

Does that come from an intuition?

I am a reasonable judge of people of their work ethic. I can tell whether a person has the right attitude, whether they're intelligent enough to follow directions and that they can create their own strategy from these directives.

Once we employ people, we maintain high morale among our team. I am the first one to put my hand up to do the not so nice jobs. If I am prepared to do something, then everyone is. This is the way I lead my team, like the Charging General on horseback in the old days. If I won't do it, I can't ask someone else to.

Have you experienced personal defeat and how did you overcome this? Was this a way you never thought possible?

It was a personal defeat when we were unable to sell our oysters. I had to find a way around this. That's when we started developing our retail outlet and our café which eventually lead to our restaurant. We completely changed the course of our business and our focus.

What keeps you motivated?

The greatest motivation is my workplace. It is the most magnificent place to work which is located out on the lake amongst the wildlife. Even on cold mornings, the sun shining quickly warms your back. It's such a joy to do what I do and to have my entire family work with me. And it is a joy to go to work every day. We are one big happy family even though we do work long hours.

What are your weaknesses?

My greatest weakness is that I am too soft. I always look at situations in role reversal. I am always the one to say, "Have a bonus, thank you for doing what you do." Much to my detriment, I give people too much money.

What are the common mistakes you see people make achieving success?

With team members, I would say one of the greatest weaknesses is not being able to assess people. This is absolutely critical to success. We have to recognize that we are human and that we can't possibly do everything ourselves.

You have to find good people for specific tasks such as chefs and front-of-house managers. You need to have the right people, otherwise, you are not going to create your business the way you want it. The biggest weakness I feel is that people are not able to make good choices when it comes to getting the right people to work for them.

How do you inspire others?

I'm the person who will say "Give me the shovel and I will dig the hole so let's just do it." I am that kind of leader and I always take that view.

Who has inspired you the most in the past?

My father had a multitude of businesses. He inspired me in two ways. One was his work ethic in that he was determined to be a success. Humans have limitations and you get into things that you don't have expertise in. He bought in a range of businesses that he didn't really have expertise in. He had to rely on people to run those businesses for him and often they let him down.

Secondly, I learned that if you want something done properly, the best thing is to do it yourself. If you try to do too many things you will spread yourself thinly, maybe fail. So you have to rely on getting good people to work with you if required.

Keep things simple and do what you do well.

Build it and they will come.
~ **From '*Field of Dreams*' movie.**

Ingo Meissner

A gourmet expert from Germany.
Cooks French and Mediterranean style food.
Head chef at The Grain Store, Melbourne.

INGO MEISSNER

What would you like other people to know about your approach to sustainability?

The sustainable approach is what The Grain Store takes a stand for. I would describe it as going back to the grassroots, going back to basics. It is a way of life.

Going back to when I grew up, my grandma went to the market or out into the garden each morning. She always cooked lunch with my dad. This was instead of going to the local supermarket, where you have no idea of what is actually fresh and in season, or what actually tastes good.

To be sustainable, we have to eat what the season offers. For us, it is what the market offers. That's what we stand for, as well as for tasting the distinction.

We don't utilize numerous added substances as we just don't have them. It's really about honesty, sincerity, and clarity without any smoke and mirrors, as they say in English.

We serve sustenance in the manner in which it was intended to be. It has to be delightful in nutritional value, solid and in a constantly scrumptious way.

This is what we wanted to deliver to our customers and to convey healthy nourishment. And we are successful at doing this.

How does a positive attitude contribute to what you do?

A positive attitude is about everything. You have to be positive, otherwise, you wouldn't be able to motivate, or guide your staff members in general.

What happens when something negative occurs? How do you confront that issue?

It's about learning from the experience. I think about teaching and really about explaining. You put yourself in their shoes.

When I became a chef, what made me tick really is about explaining what we know, why we do things the way we do, and the way we see it.

Have you ever experienced a personal defeat? What did you do to overcome this and was this in a way you never thought possible?

I always get back up. I was taught I think, keep on trying. Personally, I believe in myself.

What you put into your mind, you will achieve it. What your mind believes your body can achieve. It's about being able to. Everything happens in your heads. We let ourselves down in our heads as most of it gets done subconsciously.

It's about being able to understand. Defeats are where you learn from. You get back on the horse again.

What keeps you motivated on a daily basis?

My family and customer satisfaction are what keeps me motivated.

We started this business because we wanted to work for ourselves and make people happy. And our main focus is on happy customers in a happy family, which are our staff members.

This is a good starting point which gets you through the day. This motivates you not just for today, but for the next few weeks.

What do you consider to be your weaknesses?

I'm not a very good salesperson and I am impatient.

Apart from these, I have learned a lot over the years. You learn to adapt and adjust to the requirements of the business; and your daily requirements of life in general.

Tell me what are some of the common mistakes people make achieving success?

A common mistake people make is that they are always being too focused on money. They don't focus on creating and are only being able to see the money side of things.

Also, misunderstand the mechanics of how a business works in general. There are so many more different aspects of running a business. You have to work in a positive way to continuously operate a successful business.

You have to stay true to yourself. Don't be manipulative and don't try to be somebody that you are not going to be.

How do you inspire others?

Sharing your knowledge, your skills and mentoring.

It's the inspiration that comes naturally when people look up to you and respect you. It will just happen as a small admiration. It might be of the success of other people. Maybe they will ask themselves how we achieved it, or how was that possible?

By sharing your knowledge, your skills, and your experiences they will learn and grow themselves. It's our duty to teach the next generation to overcome daily challenges and provide them with the tools to do so.

What was the most endearing or most wow moment that you have ever had?

I would have to say that would be the birth of my son.

Prior to that, it would be being successful with the business we work in; because we love being here. We love doing what we are doing. It has always a positive force with a positive outlook.

We achieved what we wanted to achieve and we are still very happy.

Where there's a will there's a way. ~ **Proverb**

Jack Lee

Winner 2018 Chef of the Year.
Owner/chef Café Bean Smuggler, Point Cook, Victoria.

JACK LEE

What inspired you to become a chef?

In Asia, the pressure of studying is really high. I just didn't want to study. So I chose to be a chef. I wasn't very patient at the beginning and tried to avoid the study.

There was a TV drama show with a chef. So that was when I decided to become a chef in Korea only because they looked cool. Since I finished school in Korea, I wanted to explore different food culture then I decided to move to Australia which has multi-cultural cuisine.

In the beginning, I thought I should get another job. But soon started to enjoy cooking and then the study as well. I've found it is really fun and motivating a lot. Being a chef is very enjoyable.

Did your mother teach you cooking?

Not really, she's not the best cook mum. So I learned from the school which is French cuisine based school. So I'm not really good at Korean cooking, just like my mum is not.

What is the most challenging part of being a chef?

Chef's work is physically demanding. So a lot of chefs have trouble with the wrist and with standing for long periods of time. The work is physically demanding and challenging for sure. I need to keep myself both physically and mentally healthy.

Being in the kitchen the whole day does not allow much time for socializing with other people as well.

Describe a typical day.

I start at six o'clock in the morning, set up the kitchen, set up the coffee machine before the other staff come in. Then start preparing food for customers and close down the kitchen at three o'clock and finish by four o'clock and then walk away. I work seven days a week at the moment as it is the early stage of my business. I am training my staff so that I can get time off soon.

What is the best piece of advice that you have been given?

The food needs to be tasty, as well as being safe to eat. Chefs need to take responsibility and as the priority for their customers. Enjoy cooking while giving the best to the customers.

What do you hope to inspire in others?

Chefs need to study, not just stay in the kitchen, but explore and try something new to become a better chef. Cooking in a competition is such a good way to find where you are standing as a chef as well as to stay motivated.

What do you do in your time off?

I spend my time with my partner and family, is the most important thing. Try to be out from the kitchen and refresh the mind.

Do you promote yourself on social network?

I do promote my business on the social network, but not much for myself, but one day, I want to be more popular among chefs and inspire others.

What did you learn from cooking in competitions?

I learned a lot of different skills. Like a new style of plating, the different approach with ingredients and flavor pairing. I love the competitions.

Each of the chefs has different skills and knowledge. Some use traditional skills to cook while some other chefs using modern techniques with the same ingredients.

When cooking in competitions, I try to cook simple and perfect. Over-complicating a dish in a competition is the best way to lose points.

Why do you think you were chosen as Chef of the Year 2018?

Because I had a few competition experiences over the last couple of years and learned from judges and other competitors on how to win a cooking competition.

"Keep it simple and focus on the main ingredient" was the best piece of advice that I have been given from other judges.

At the end of each round of Chef of the Year 2018 competition, I tried to get as many feedbacks as I could get from judges and tried to bring that into the next round. This enabled me to improve my performance in the Grand Final.

Other competitors were great chefs from all around Australia and they surely inspired me with what they have done in the competition. Probably the only reason I could win was the previous competition experience.

What is the key recipe for success?

Always push hard to be better.

There is no excuse for not giving the best.

Do not compromise with quality.

Be open-minded to any opinions and advises.

Please share one of your experiences working as a chef?

My first job in Australia, I was kicked out from the kitchen in my second week of working because I couldn't understand what the chef was saying and made him upset.

That was my worst experience in the kitchen but at the same time the most valuable lesson I received.

Communication is the most important thing in the kitchen, especially in a high-pressure environment. Any chefs in Australia who don't have English as their first language, please study hard. No matter how good the cooking skill is, there is no chance to move up without strong communication skills.

What are the important skills to be a great chef?

Enjoying cooking.

If a chef doesn't enjoy cooking, people will taste the lack of passion.

Do you have a mentor?

Lachlan Colwill from Hentley Farm Restaurant in Barossa Valley, South Australia.

I was just a random Asian boy, knocked on the kitchen door and he accepted me as a part of the team.

He promoted me to manage the kitchen and gave me great opportunities to improve not only cooking skills but also socializing in the kitchen and managing a big team of chefs with confidence.

My cooking style is surely inspired by his cuisine.

Enjoy and give your best.

Jason Mizzen

Winner of Australia's Best Gourmet Pie 2017.

JASON MIZZEN

Please share how you started your cooking journey.

I grew up enjoying food. In the school holidays, I did baking and cooking with my mother and was inspired by her. So I chose cooking at school, while my mates were doing woodwork and metalwork. I enjoyed working with my hands. I especially loved the fiddly details of cake decorating and being creative, so I decided to be a pastry chef.

I wanted to be a drummer and a musician. My father said that it's good as a passion, but you don't always have a steady income playing music. That drove me to get a trade.

At high school, then after leaving school, I worked at a bakery for free. I was approached by the owner of another bakery, so I changed bakeries to do an apprenticeship.

I have now been at Brighton's Best Bakehouse in Hobart for 18 years and managing it at 21. The owners gave me the creative freedom to do everything. They let me experiment with different recipes and go for it. They gave me opportunities to compete in competitions, where I have been winning medals for over a decade.

How does a positive attitude contribute to what you do?

Always pick out the positives. Anyone who is negative is always going to draw negatives to them. Find the positivity in anything you do and really love what you do. Find something you really enjoy and are passionate about. That's always going to be a positive experience. When you are positive toward something, positive things come back to you.

What are your greatest professional strengths?

I am very hard working, which my working parents instilled in me. I am a bit of a perfectionist and like things to be done the right way. When I get focused on an idea, I am driven to achieve it.

Have you ever experienced personal defeat and how did you overcome it?

I remember I was doing the course to be a trainer and assessor in the baking industry. I was working on a presentation to give to the class. In the presentation, I had to work out percentages and explain how I develop pastry. My head was so full with this information I had been working on, that I got frazzled. I had forgotten how to do it! My wife told me to go outside, take a walk and to clear my head and to step away from it. I went outside and stepped back from it and it all came back to me straight away.

There are barriers in life that can overcome you. You think you can't get past them. Take a step back and look at it from a different perspective.

What keeps you motivated on a daily basis?

My motivation comes from having balance in my life.

I am a musician and my motivation and success come from my hobbies and my music. When I have had a big day at work and feeling stressed, I play my drums or have band practice with my mates. That takes all my focus away from any stress issues and I can return to work the next day feeling clear headed. You need a release and I have that release when I play music, especially with my friends.

What do you consider to be your weakness?

My temper! I like things to be done a certain way. I find it really hard to get people to do things the way I want them to be done. It's not so much my temper, but I usually find if you want something done properly and done well, I have to do it myself. This is something that I need to work on. I have to believe in the people around me and find ways to manage people better.

What are some of the common mistakes people make achieving success?

You need to focus on the positive. People who achieve success have been knocked down and have to pick themselves back up and keep trying. This takes heart. Some of the most successful people say to achieve success it was due to their failures. The fear of failure may be what holds people back achieving success.

How do you inspire others?

Always treat people with respect and treat them the way you would like to be treated.

I try to lead by example. With my staff, I show them how I like things done. I strive to do everything to the best of my ability and do things the right way. They follow on from that and gain inspiration. It's showing people that you can succeed if you believe in yourself and work hard.

Who has inspired you the most?

I get inspiration from my family who all inspire me to do well. I have always wanted to make my parents and my family proud. People say that once you have kids your life changes. It's very true. Now that I'm a father I'm inspired by my kids and want to inspire them to achieve success in their future.

I also draw inspiration from my friends. They are supportive with my success in winning pie competitions. Also Michael Jordan and Michael

Jackson who have achieved greatness inspire me.

What's your vision for the future?

I am qualified as a trainer and assessor and hope to teach apprentices at TAFE level. I want to inspire young apprentices and mentor them; to encourage them to enter competitions and to strive to be the best.

Don't ever think you know everything. You can learn from someone who's just beginning. There's always something to learn no matter how much you think you know.

I like to inspire people to push themselves to be better, as this would benefit the whole trade. What I am truly passionate about has pushed me to be the best. That's my mission.

You can't do your best when you doubt yourself. If you don't believe in yourself who will? ~ **Michael Jackson**

Jude Mayall

Native bush food expert and author.
CEO of Outback Chef.

JUDE MAYALL

What is your background?

My family has been country people for generations with orchards and vineyards. Like all country people, making preserves, baking and cooking was an important part of our daily life. I learned a lot from my mother who cooked for the family and also catered professionally. Both food and art have been my motivation for my job. I've been involved in Australian Aboriginal art since the late '80s and learned about Indigenous food and culture through their amazing artworks. I remember asking an elderly lady artist once about her painting. She explained about the bush tomato, this really opened my eyes. My journey into native food was both a logical and passionate progression.

What values are important to you?

I come from generations of Australians. What this land supplies are really important, not only for me but for future generations. We have to honor the land and what it produces and educate people on how to use its native food.

If we're eating what the land provides, it's definitely a healthier option. The food from our native soils has an abundance of nutrients. These are not only important for our health and lifestyle, but also our emotional wellness which I believe needs that direct connection to the land.

What is most challenging with your work?

It has been educating people to use native foods. Chefs are now embracing Australian natives and incorporating them into their menus.

This is exciting. People really want to know where their food comes from, where it's been harvested and the benefits. It's come full circle.

Do you put any procedures in place for the future?

On a day to day basis it's running a business; pay the bills and feeding people. Where I want to go is working more with remote communities with food harvesting and value adding. These are the procedures I now have in place.

What is your most exciting wow factor product?

I sell native herbs and spices. The 'wow factor' is how well our native edibles combine with imported products. Australia is such a multicultural society with most of our food coming from Europe, the Middle East, and Asia. I find it exciting that our natives mingle so well with other cuisines.

Our chefs are creating amazing dishes incorporating Australian flavors to create something that is uniquely Australian. That's the 'wow factor' for me.

What are your strengths?

My strength is my background in Indigenous art. It gives me a good understanding of where the food comes from and the cultural significance behind the food. This helps me tell the story when I'm giving talks and also when I'm creating products.

I am a good 'people person'. I talk to lots of culinary students and young chefs. I love color. I absolutely love different flavors, value adding, creating recipes and creating products.

What would you consider your weaknesses?

Bookkeeping, facts, and figures! I have a great bookkeeper and accountant who keep me on track. I am a challenge for them.

What are the misconceptions around bush food?

In the past, people have related bush food to only belonging in the outback and around campfires, but this has changed dramatically in the past few years.

People can now go out to dine and may have a dish that contains strawberry gum or lemon myrtle with native pepperberries. Diners are starting to see that natives are sophisticated in fine dining. They are being used to their best advantage and it's all happening now.

If you were stuck on an island, what food would you want the most?

I would really want lemons and limes. I like things like bread and rice dishes. I'm not a vegetarian, but I do eat a lot of plant-based dishes. I love working with vegetables because vegetables are the star on any dish.

How do you initiate strategic plans?

Planning has to start in my head. I have to actually see and work things out in my head first. I work out food colors, flavors and taste this way. Once I've got it in my head and I feel confident, then I write it down and work with it.

Would you like to share the longest rabbit hole that you've been down?

This is sharing the knowledge of native food to non-Indigenous people and getting people to take our native Indigenous food on board in their day to day lives, in their pantry, and on their menus.

What weird food combinations do you really enjoy?

Strawberry gum is a really interesting flavor. It's a leaf that grows on a big tree which is dried. It's got a unique and beautiful sort of berry, aromatic Australian bush type flavor. It can be really bizarre with the wrong food, but with the right food, it tastes absolutely gorgeous.

I made a tea with strawberry gum rose and blackberry and then I combined it with Australian grown green tea. Weird combination, but it works wonderfully well.

What always cheers you up?

People's happiness and excitement when they discover and try new native flavors for the first time, it makes what I do all worthwhile. Our natives tick all the boxes.

What motivational quotes keep you inspired?

You keep moving forward. If digging one hole isn't working, start digging in another to find one that does work. You have to stay with what you are doing right. It's not a matter of giving up. It's a matter of pursuing what you feel is right. It comes down to "Giving up is not an option." To move forward you find another way, especially if it's something you believe in.

There are many paths you can take to reach the same end.

Karen Borg

Cheesemaker & CEO of Willowbrae award-winning range of artisan goats milk cheese.

KAREN BORG

Can you expand on why you started making goats cheese?

We couldn't get good quality cheese as most were aged imported cheese. Having a property, I had a brainstorm as little Capricorns do. Without telling my husband I borrowed his ute to purchase a mother and baby goat and a book on how to make cheese. By the time I got home, they were screaming their lungs out! That was 20 years ago now.

A friend gave me the springboard to sell my cheese at markets. So we worked for weeks and weeks trying to get a mass product together. On opening night I couldn't believe the response after selling all our products. Later entering into the Melbourne Royal Show and receiving two silver medals. So that was our launching platform.

How did you get your kitchen setup to actually manufacture the cheese?

Back then it was run by the local council and was later approved by the Food Authority. We just knew we had to build proper kitchen manufacturing facilities. Initially, we could actually test the waters making the product in an approved council kitchen. These days you need to be fully approved with the Food Authority.

What is the most challenging part of your job?

The goats are the most challenging. I think that's why you don't see a lot of people actually taking on goat cheese making. They are creatures of habit. They are quite particular in the way that they need to be looked after.

Do you like to have things carefully planned or do you prefer to go along with the flow?

I tend to go with the flow these days. When we first started off, I had everything planned. But when you are dealing with livestock and natural things in general and raising a family, you learn very quickly to start to go with the flow.

What values are the most important to you?

My family. You know it is great having a family around, space and being at home. Working on the farm brought our family quite close, especially working 24/7 with each other as well.

How do you cope with the business side?

I used to do business management before I started cheesemaking. You had to be so strict and regulated with the paperwork. I hate that work now. There is always running after animals and cheese to be done. You can catch up with it later on.

What is your favorite part of your job?

I love developing new products and getting the feedback straight away from our customers as we sell directly at the growers market and to restaurants. When we first started, our cheese was a super fresh style, but we have now developed a mature range. This is due to the feedback we receive and the Australian palate has changed. People are requesting a stronger flavor. Getting feedback has been crucial in the development of our business.

It is better to fail in originality than to succeed in imitation.
~ Herman Melville

Luke Florence

Luke's passion for cooking and travel took him to USA, Central America and Buenos Aires where he did a Diploma of Culinary Arts in patisserie and bakery. Since returning to Australia he became a vegetarian chef, with a motivating force to make healthy food taste delicious!

LUKE FLORENCE

Why did you decide to become a chef?

Cooking was a hobby. I moved to Sydney when I was 17 with friends and they were all chefs, so I worked in kitchens. I have a worldly heart and I wanted to travel the world. With cooking, I had the opportunity to pursue my profession as well as travel.

I have a passion to make healthy food taste good. What people define as good food isn't always healthy, as people want something that satisfies their taste buds.

What is most important to you?

I believe it's important to source food that's environmentally friendly. It has to be well farmed and have good nutrition. It has to be fresh food, organic and biodynamic where possible, with little impact on the environment.

What is the most challenging part of your job?

To be a great chef, you have to be passionate. This takes up a large portion of my life and my energy. The biggest challenge is balancing between yoga, meditation and breathing work; and being a father, a husband, and a chef.

This has been more challenging since becoming a father. Before I had just enough time for my partner and I could balance things. Now that I have a child, I have to give him an appropriate amount of energy and teach him to grow into a balanced human being. It's difficult to balance that with the demand of being a good chef.

What is the most amazing dish you created?

The one that pops in my head, which was a mind blower, was a silken tofu dish with smoked dashi broth. It was really good quality tofu and a beautiful broth – something that I hadn't experienced before.

How would you spend an unexpected three day paid leave?

I would head to the mountains with my son, my wife and my dog and sleep under the stars, enjoying nature.

Have you any tips that you can share?

Don't let difficult times get you down. They are part of life. When you come out on the other side, you will have learned great lessons from the experience.

What is the most amazing place you have been in?

I spent a summer living in virgin forest with friends on Vancouver Island, British Columbia. We lived under a tree which had an eagle with its young. We watched the eagles grow over the summer. We had encounters with bears, nature, big beautiful trees and the energy of the forest. It was the most amazing time in my life.

What have you experienced that you wouldn't recreate and how have you grown from that?

It started in the mid-teens as a downward spiral on recreational drugs, followed by the death of my best friend. I couldn't deal with what was going on in my life. I hit rock bottom where I was happy to die, or I had the option to crawl my way out from there. I didn't know which way I wanted to go. Then my mother died and that was my catalyst for change.

I started to crawl my way out from that hole until I got to a place where I saw the unhappiness within me. I looked at it to see where it was coming from. I went through a transformative state, which led to me becoming spiritual and understanding my nature in a completely different way.

I came from a place where I didn't have any love for myself; therefore I didn't have any love for anything around me. The realization that I gained from this was that if I can't love myself, I can't love anything else around me. I realized that if I learned to love myself, it would mean I'd have a love for everything. It became a mission to explore how I could allow that to happen in my life.

I worked quite diligently for a number of years, which led me to the place on Vancouver Island where I spent several months in nature. This brought me to a place where I felt love for every little thing around me. I felt love for myself and acceptance and an understanding of everything that had happened in my life.

I could actually see why these things happened and that there is good when bad things happen. If you are wise along the path; you come to great things.

And what are your strengths and weaknesses?

My strength is that I am a relatively compassionate and understanding person. It's important to give people individual creative expression. One of my strengths is to create food and to allow people their creative expression to influence the dish we are making. It makes them feel that they are a part of the kitchen. This creates a family environment and a place where people feel they are part of what's going on.

My weakness is that I am unorganized and a little slow and sometimes I need a kick up the backside. This can be seen as a weakness, but it can be seen as a strength, as I don't get too stressed.

That is important because I understand that the best way to teach people and change things is by your own actions. Hence this quote:

Be the change you want to see in the world.
~ **Mahatma Gandhi**

Luke Mangan

Luke is an Australian chef and restaurateur in Sydney and at sea on P&O cruise ships. He is the Consulting chef for Virgin Australia Business Class. He produces gourmet products and is the co-founder of the Hospitality Awards program: 'The Inspired Series' and Australia's 'Appetite for Excellence' plus an award-winning author.

LUKE MANGAN

What processes do you put into place to support staff coming into the hospitality industry?

In 2004 we started a program called 'Appetite for Excellence', which is a National Awards program to attract the best people in Australia's food industry. This is targeted toward young chefs, waiters and restaurateurs to celebrate and nurture young talent and the future of our hospitality industry.

This program encourages, motivates and educates people within our industry. Our aim is to keep them involved in it. We assist them to understand the pitfalls, as well as the good times and bad times, within hospitality. We have the wonderful support of great chefs from Peter Gilmore, Ross Lusted to Guy Rossi.

In 2015, we started another program with Sir Richard Branson called 'The Inspired Series'. This is a Development program for TAFE students and young chefs to reduce the dropout rates while they are doing their apprentices. This has involved developing a Question and Answer series from successful people within the industry.

We launched this with Sir Richard, by asking him questions of how he got started with all the ups and downs that he experienced. We then moved to people who have succeeded in our industry who are doing well. It's all about telling the story about how they persisted and kept going despite their ups and downs. It is about understanding and providing career advice and support within the hospitality industry.

How do you instill the right mindset for your staff to excel?

We have got a good culture and we love what we do. For me, what I do is not a job. It is something I do and I really enjoy.

You have to be passionate about what you do and you have to enjoy the workspace. You cannot take things too seriously either. I like to be relaxed, friendly and approachable. It helps that you know 'top of the ladder' in our company structure and that everyone within it is approachable.

We know we will all sit down together and have the glass of wine at the end of the week. Our team has many different interests.

We have a gym club, which we fund, where our team can go to the gym for an hour a week, or go together as a group. It's a very relaxed atmosphere.

What is your best way of leading the team?

It is important not to micromanage and as it is far more important to set a good example and be a leader.

The relationship between us has to be open and honest. If there is a problem, I have to know about it and how to work together to fix it and make sure it doesn't happen again. The essence is to empower the team to make decisions and move on from issues.

How do you create a work and life balance?

When you work in the hospitality industry, you don't conform to the 9-5 working day or even to the standard 40-hour work week. I love this industry so much and I cannot think of doing anything else. It can seem an impossible task to achieve a balance between work and life when your work is your life.

Over the years I have adopted some habits into my daily life, so I prioritize my time – which isn't easy. I have to find effective ways of managing my day, to ensure I don't end up working overtime! I have to get enough sleep – as it is easy to forget how important a good night's sleep is, for us to perform our work and function well the next day.

A healthy body means a healthy mind. Eating healthily and doing regular exercise are great stress-busters.

And don't forget to ask for help and support. If you are working to your maximum and feeling stressed, then do not hesitate to delegate. Ask someone to help you out until you find your groove again.

Two things define us. Our patience when we have nothing and our attitude when we have everything. ~ **George Bernard Shaw**

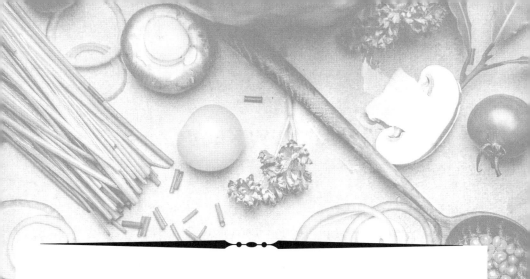

Matthew Kemp

A distinguished Michelin international chef career winning lots of awards and industry respect. Executive chef at Kingscliff Beach Bowls Club.

MATTHEW KEMP

What are your greatest professional strengths?

My strength is my ability to read people in the kitchen. It is a really important aspect of being part of a team. Understanding their strengths and weaknesses and how to get the best out of each person.

Being a good Executive Head Chef requires you to be a psychologist. We are a mixed bunch of individuals. In the kitchen and in the hospitality industry you really do have to understand this. My strength is my leadership style within the kitchen.

Think about a time when you encountered a personal defeat and how did this affect you?

I got demoted from two Chef Hat's to one Chef Hat in the Australian Good Food Guide, for my restaurant in Sydney.

It was one of the most heart-wrenching things that I ever experienced. I was crying and was absolutely deflated. I had never felt anything like that before. In hindsight, it was just a piece of paper. I vowed to get it back the next year and we did.

I put my head down and worked my backside off by motivating my team in a positive way. I was determined that I would get this back if I put my all into it.

We lost a lot of money going down to a one Chef Hat that year, as it is financially driven too.

What keeps you motivated on a daily basis?

My love for cooking and my passion is creating dishes.

The reason I get up in the morning is for my family. I wasn't around earlier for my children because I worked so much in my restaurant. So I didn't have the time I should have had with them. I have found a way to change that with the recent additions to my family.

And what do you consider to be your weaknesses?

I am not great with confrontation. It is definitely not one of my strongest points. I always have to work at this. It's definitely one of my weaknesses.

How do you handle confrontation?

Not fantastically, but the older I get the stronger I become. I understand that confrontation is not about being aggressive. It's about getting your point across and the reason why you're doing it. I am still learning.

So tell me what are some of the common mistakes people make achieving success?

We don't look back enough on the successes that we've had. We have to realize that success is what people enjoy. When we win accolades for the previous year, it is because of what we serve. Looking at what you did and learning from it, makes that a perfect experience.

Make that really strong and don't forget it, because that's what people in this industry do. They don't look back at their successes and work to strengthen those points. This is definitely what we do.

I've certainly learned a lot from the last seven or eight years because I went bankrupt.

I have gathered a lot of knowledge along the way from people I have worked with. You must learn from your mistakes. If you don't learn from your mistakes, you are going to make them again.

How do you inspire others?

The way I inspire others is with encouragement. In essence, chefs have to be inspired to create and to do things better is purely through encouragement.

I have to be a good leader to inspire others. If I can do the pot washing, anyone can do the pot washing. I don't just stand at the front waving my clipboard around. I feel to inspire is to encourage. Great leadership is a sense of getting in and doing the job, as well as showing others that you can do it.

You have to not just talk; you have to be able to do it. In my industry that's so important because there are so many talkers and not enough doers. Younger people have to be inspired. They have to be able to see that what I'm asking them to do, is what I do. I have seen head chefs and executives that say "Do this, do that," with no idea how to actually do it.

Who inspired you the most in the past?

There are two chefs who inspired me the most in my career.

There is Liam Tomlin, whom I worked with in three different restaurants. He got me to go back to England to work in a Michelin Star restaurant. He said, "To get more experience and go back and learn more." It was one of the best things I ever did.

The job I got, by pure chance in London, was with Phil Howard. I learned everything I have been cooking for the past ten years from him. He taught me how to cook again. It was one of the most inspirational times in my working life working with them. These two chefs definitely inspired me.

What was the most crowning moment in your life?

I got five of them as I have five kids.

Phil Howard taught me that there is no point in being some flash chef putting food onto a plate if you first don't know how it's going to taste like as a full meal. This defines how well you can write and formulate a complete menu for your guests.

To know how to cook well, you must first know how to dine.

Neil Abrahams

Hospitality Consultant, Principal Knives Edge Consultancy.
Founding President of the Australian Culinary Federation ACT Chapter.
Competing in Australian National Culinary Team for 6 years and co-captained the 2008 Culinary Olympic Team.
Melbourne Culinary Challenge Chef of the Year 2006, in 2009 and 2011 including numerous gold medals plus Food Services Australia's Chef of the Year 2012 and 2013.
Elected National President of the Australian Culinary Federation 2014-present.

NEIL ABRAHAMS

How did you become a consultant chef?

I have worked in this industry for over 30 years and had several companies ask me to represent their products. I took an opportunity to work as an industry consultant, based on 60 days a year. Then I built up my own clients from companies who had approached me previously.

My work is international and spans across USA, Asia and the Middle East, with 85% of what I do being in Asia. I have had lots of mentors along the way, so here I am four years into being an industry consultant.

Why did you take the role of President of the Australian Culinary Federation?

I have had a very lucky career path. We are masters of our own destinies based on the decisions we make. I always chose positions where I learn.

When you become the boss, you become a teacher instead of a student. I made a decision when I was younger to not take on an executive role too soon. This was off the back of executive chefs working in hotels. They kept saying, "Don't be in such a hurry, stay back and learn as much as you can." I didn't take a first supervisory role as Chef De Partie until I was 26. Many people are a head chef now at 23 or 24.

I pursued culinary competitions when I was younger. These competitions developed my skills and really cemented them into my DNA. I was fortunate enough to be selected for the National Culinary Olympic team in 2004 and I co-captained the team in 2008. The Australian Culinary Federation is the foundation for these competitions throughout Australia.

I have been given lots of opportunities and I wanted to give these back. In 2002 I set up the Australian Capital Territory (ACT) Chapter of the Australian Culinary Federation. I was the founding President. I became a board member of the National Association, then I was Secretary and then I ran as President in 2014.

I want to encourage young chefs and we have held over 127 events across the country. We did everything from social networking events, through to workshops and working through TAFE Colleges. Our aim is to improve standards through competitions, with the global participation of Worldchefs.

What is the best way to lead your team?

It is easy to be the boss; however, our bosses are often formed through lack of experience, guidance, and mentorship. The best way to lead a team is to be a leader. That is something you have to learn. Anybody can be the boss, but it's rare to be a good leader.

What process is in place to support new chefs coming into the industry?

The Australian Culinary Federation is not a lobbyist group. We spent years gaining seats on industry reference councils and committees. This is managed by Skills IQ, on behalf of the Federal Government. Their role is to improve Australian National training packages. We have set up education committees and subcommittees within this national body to look at, review and consult with the industry.

We also work with high schools encouraging kids to take on a trade, rather than take the educational or tertiary path. The Government put most of its funding into tertiary and further education. They don't allocate much money into trades and encouraging people into Vocational Education

Training. We work within this space.

We have one paid person in the association and we have 60 volunteers working on projects. This is a testament to what the Australian Culinary Federation does.

What is the best business advice you have been given?

Keep a calm head at all times as the chef in me can get heated. Thinking things through is easy for a chef, as we are naturally passionate and artistic people, who sit back, listen and analyze.

Chefs are their own worst enemies. We do most of our business with a cup of coffee and a cigarette on a milk crate out the back of the kitchen. We are not going to change this perception until we learn how to perform in the boardroom and in the corporate world. This is not going to happen overnight, as we accept that we work within a corporate environment.

What has been your crowning glory?

Besides getting married and the birth of my children, professionally I represent Australia at an elite level. Memorable moments come from watching achievements. One side of me would say it is representing Australia, the other side is definitely watching the people I have trained succeed in the industry. These certainly have been most rewarding.

What is your vision for the future?

I have a new role now as Continental Director for the Pacific Rim. I sit on the Worldchefs board and we view the hospitality industry.

Australia is better off than other countries around the Pacific. For me, it is being able to share and work within these committees and associations in the Pacific. We assist them to establish and stabilize their committees because they are in fragile environments.

The main income of these countries is Hospitality and Tourism. We assist young chefs to gain skills on a local level so that they are less reliance on expats coming in and running their businesses for them. We work to stabilize the skills of young people so that they gain experience. This is where I am heading in the future, to assist the less fortunate in the industry.

Service is an extension of the mise en place. ~ **Gary Farrell**

Cook well, eat well, live well.

Paul Rifkin

Paul Rifkin is a chef who is passionate about food, provenance, and education. He is a committee member of the Australian Culinary Federation, mentors and judges chefs and apprentices for competitions, career, and scholarships, worked at the Sydney Olympics and has taught at TAFE colleges.

PAUL RIFKIN

How did you get into cooking?

I started off working as a TV technician and became a chef by accident. I was a kitchen hand, washing dishes for my brother who was an apprentice chef and I started helping out in the kitchen. Before I knew it, I was cooking. I basically learned on the job. Then I went from leadership in one catering outlet to another, always landing harder roles. This culminated as Executive Chef in a large club with eight restaurants, a convention center, hotel, fitness center and golf club serving 13,000 meals a week.

Why did you become a consultant chef?

With 40 years of knowledge behind me and 30 years working as an Executive Chef, I decided that I didn't want to be in charge of 150 staff, so I had to find something to do. The best way to do this was to use my knowledge and help others to solve their problems. Hence I became a consultant chef.

I use social media to let people know what I am doing. I moved to an area away from where my normal network was. I had to make sure that the people knew where I was and when I was there. With LinkedIn, Instagram and Facebook, I grew a very strong network.

With consulting you have to believe in yourself. If you go in scared and you have no confidence, people won't trust your ability. From my point-of-view, the most important thing is to have confidence in yourself and what you've done in the past. If you believe it, it'll happen. There will always be trepidation and this is not fear.

What was your most defining moment?

Recently I summited the top of Mount Kilimanjaro during a blizzard.

It was minus 20 degree Celsius and blowing a gale. I walked some 18 hours that day. Once I achieved this, I knew I had to change what I do. I had done a lot of things and climbed a lot of mountains, but I had not climbed a mountain in minus 20 degrees Celsius, straight up through 1000 meters of snow, being blinded by it and still kept going up to nearly 6000 meters altitude, not much oxygen there!

On that trip, I took a photo of a leaping leopard which was published around the world in National Geographic, newspapers and magazines and on social media. It hit over 100 million likes and shares.

This forced me to find what was inside myself. This is why I resigned from a long-term job, as I didn't want to follow anybody else's plans or rules.

What are your greatest successes?

When we first got married, we bought a house. Then the next year we bought a yacht. The next year we bought a yacht that cost as much as the house. This is because we decided that we were going to do things differently. We weren't going to follow any rules.

Our kids grew up on yachts while other people's kids grew up playing Nintendo. Our kids learned to be creative and they all turned out to be beautiful adults. Everybody has a different path.

What are your biggest challenges?

As a consultant, I identify the issues that businesses have. I look at the shortfalls, missed opportunities and things of concern. Each time I walk into a place, I have three days to analyze everything that happens during the peak of service.

This is exciting and I have to get everybody to work with me during that period of time. My biggest challenge is getting to know a whole new crew of people and getting them to trust me enough to get inside their heads. I interview people like the general manager, the owner or the

CEO and other people involved in the management chain.

I have to extrapolate out of them what is missing; what they would do to change it, and I have to ask them if they are the right person for the job. I go into analyze everything and it gets quite messy. When I finish, I have 20 to 30 pages of notes, drawings, and pictures that I have to put into a report which is intelligible and worthwhile. It's like throwing confetti into the air. It then takes me 10 or 12 hours to put all this information into a 15 or 20-page report.

I have also had major emotional things happen in the past, but these rarely affect my work. If you go in feeling weak, the team sees it and takes advantage of it. It's lonely at the top, but the view's great.

What are your plans for the future?

We recently moved up from the south. My wife and I have changed our lives and everything about the way we operate. We are spending a year looking around new areas. We are deciding whether to get a farm or another property; whether we get a bus and keep traveling; or whether we go and live overseas. We have a year of discovery to do this, which is pretty exciting.

I am currently consulting, doing implementations and speaking at conferences. I have a lot of strings to my bow. I am a photographer and I design commercial kitchens as well.

Life is full of things that happen. Everything that happens in life creates the rest of your life. How you handle it and your approach to it (before and after), is what determines where you're going to be and how high you're going to go.

You trip, you fall over, you bloody your nose and you bounce back higher.

Sarah Wheeler

Founder of Puremelt Chocolate Byron Bay.

SARAH WHEELER

Why did you become a chocolatier?

I consulted a professor of Nutritional Medicine as a mature mum and with some health issues. He lectures around Australia and has taught many doctors who specialize in Nutritional Medicine. He advised me to change my diet to the Paleo diet.

He said to eat nuts and seeds, meat and fish, fruit and vegetables, to take certain supplements and to eat 50 grams of 85% cacao chocolate per day. He advised that this chocolate had to be low in sugar and of the best quality. So I went to look for what was available in terms of organic chocolate and low sugar, but could not find good quality.

I knew how to make chocolate, so I developed a recipe and started eating 50 grams a day. I didn't feel deprived on this diet. I ate leftover casserole for breakfast, salads for lunch and after lunch, I would have two or three of my chocolates. It felt very indulgent and my health got better.

Friends and family were enjoying my chocolates. Then our family finances got low, so I approached the lady running Mullumbimby Farmers Market and the Summer Food Festival to sell my chocolates at the market. That was eight years ago.

What values are most important to you?

My business and personal ethics and not compromising the product in any way are both my strengths and values. I use the finest ingredients that I can get. They are all fair trade, organic and ethically sourced to make the best chocolate possible. I really enjoy this challenge and I am very passionate about what I do.

What is the most challenging?

Balancing the books! I started my business on a shoestring. To set up the business, I borrowed $5000 from a friend which I paid back in the first year. I had to change my car and get a mobile freezer. I wanted the business to be sustainable. In retrospect, I realize now that it actually helped not to have any extra borrowings as I was not able to waste money on any mistakes in the early days of business.

Have you put procedures in place for the future?

I'm starting to do that now with more planning. I started this from passionate enthusiasm. It was about making chocolates, and what I had to do today then next day. Now I'm looking further ahead.

I have definitely gone with the flow in the past. I have to do more planning now and of course, listen to my inner voice and my intuition.

Describe your creative process

Most of my recipes and success happened the first time around. There is a sense when I am creating on how to create it. I seem to get it right the first time. I try a new flavor or add new ingredients from an inner sense. It's to my taste, but may not be everybody's taste. It seems to come together.

I used to have a sweet tooth. The chocolate I make is 85% cacao. I don't use much-refined sugar. I use vanilla to counteract the bitterness of the cacao, so it's very smooth. Also, I use coconut sugar instead of cane sugar in my products.

How did you know what products to use?

One of my sons had food intolerances when he was younger, which included wheat, sugar, and eggs. I was motivated to provide him with deliciousness in his food, without irritating him. So I was used to looking at ingredients on labels and making alternative options for him.

How did you feel when you got your recipe right?

Very excited and really happy. I have developed other products with chocolate. I created a Paleo Vegan chocolate chip cookie which is really popular. This feels so good, especially as people are really enjoying it.

Do you have any tips that you can share?

Use the best ingredients you can source.

Watch the movie 'Like Water for Chocolate' – there is a wonderful scene in that movie depicting how the lady felt as she was preparing food. This is really important.

Fortunately, I'm pretty much a happy person. I believe to make good food you need to have good thoughts whilst creating and preparing.

Have you experienced any difficult challenges?

The most challenging for me has been going from financial abundance to being challenged financially. The positive is that I had to have a sustainable business right from the start.

Now my challenge is to make my gourmet products available to the wider public; so they appreciate a delicious product that is also super healthy.

A mind once stretched by a new idea never regains its original dimensions. ~ **Oliver Wendell Holmes Jr.**

Shane Delia

Shane Delia is a chef and restaurateur of Middle Eastern cuisine, TV presenter, author, charity ambassador of prominent sporting clubs, charities and Mercedes Benz.

SHANE DELIA

What values are important to you?

Respect for people, culture, produce, and history. If you don't respect the past, then you are living in a limited world.

I have been fortunate to grow up in a loving Maltese family. Respect was everything. The biggest challenge is people who don't have respect. I'm a cook who does not compete with my industry or try to change the world through cooking. We are just trying to cook our food and offer great experiences. People are taking notice and respect what we are doing, which is flattering.

My greatest goal is to find balance in life. Balance not just for me, but for my team, ensuring that they have the opportunity to live well. Personally, spending time with my family and loved ones, but most of all ensuring I have enough time for me.

What's the most challenging part of your job?

Staying focused on goals, the journey I am on, and when pathways change. I believe you can't set foundation pillars of life when you start cooking. Your views change, and life experiences help you grow. Staying on track with important issues isn't easy. Society tells us, "We need to be better; if you want more you have to grow; that greed is good; and that you have to divide and conquer, irrespective of who falls."

You have to stay focused on what you believe in and be brave enough to stand alone against popular thinking. Now with television and media profiles being big business in food, staying grounded isn't easy.

Temptation, greed, and lust are around every corner and this can be too much to deal with. Lines become blurred when people start recognizing you as a 'celebrity' and not a chef. You have to stay focused on what defines.

What do you do to stay focused?

I connect with my wife, my brother, my sister and dad, with my friends and the community I am a part of. This includes my connection with my team. I love my team. I love the people that we work with, as they devote their lives to our unified dream. Connections are really important. I am a weak person and I need strong people around me. I also spend a lot of time on my personal mental and physical health. I am a firm believer in controlling the controllable.

Do you do this consciously or unconsciously?

I look at what I've done subconsciously and consciously. I have done things unconsciously that have had a major impact on my life. I take time to reflect every day on my day and try to find ways how I can improve. When necessary I take counsel from people I trust to find ways on how I can remain strong and positive.

What is your connection with Middle Eastern food and Maltese food?

Maltese food has a deep connection and history with the Middle East. We were first colonized by the Phoenicians with over 50% of our language being Arabic. My love for Malta and for our culinary ancestry was rekindled by my wife who is of Lebanese descent. Her family reminded me so much of my family and our similar cultures.

Traveling through North Africa and the Middle East, I reconnected to stories of my upbringing and flavors I grew up with through my grandparents. My culinary ancestry defines me as a cook. However, when deciding to open my restaurant I believed Maltese cuisine wasn't diverse enough to establish myself in a Maltese restaurant. So, I embraced my Phoenician ancestry and looked to the Middle East to launch my crusade to define what Maltese food could be.

I have recently been appointed a member of the Maltese Government Advisory Board, Council of Maltese Living Abroad and now have great relationships with producers, hoteliers and the government there. The Prime Minister is a personal friend and we have dreams to redefine the culinary landscape of Malta through produce, imagination, and history.

Do you like everything carefully planned or do you prefer to go with the flow?

Structure for me is imperative. Every second of my day is planned to be able to achieve what I need to achieve. I have over a hundred staff, they, in turn, have families. They all rely on me to make good decisions to ensure there's food on the table for all of our families.

I am reactive when unplanned issues arise. Now I am focused and conscious enough to sit back and assess those issues to see if they may be opportunities and if they are in line with what we want to achieve.

Who taught you the business?

It's something I taught myself. I left school at a young age without a university education. My dad came to Australia when I was 18 years old with nothing but a dream of living a better life. So many people sacrificed everything to give me this opportunity. I will never let them down!

The most important lesson I have learned is about building a strong diverse community and network. Surround yourself with positive people who love you, who are smarter and successful in their own fields. Really get to know them and some of their brilliance will rub off on you.

Have you any regrets?

I had personal experiences I regret, which have impacted on my loved ones. I have learned about myself which made me stronger.

The only thing professionally that didn't work out was the business partnership with a good friend. We had a couple of restaurants together and aren't in business anymore. This left me feeling defeated because I lost the friendship for a long time. Had I not gone through that, I wouldn't have had the motivation to make myself a better person and learn from this experience.

If you can turn a negative into a positive, look at it as a learning experience.

What is the most amazing dish you have cooked?

Every week we create two or three new dishes with so many different styles. It may be a simple dessert such as Jerusalem artichokes, roasted and turned into ice-cream; or a cake of carob, cinnamon molasses, cinnamon and Baharat, burnt orange and a tahini caramel. These dishes really define our genre in Middle Eastern food.

How do you inspire creativity?

I am unbelievably inspired. When I've eaten something raw and said: "Wow, how can I take that to the next level or how to harness that?" It's the emotion you feel when you eat a product that inspires. Sometimes I am inspired historically or by a story, which I take and create something that's my own.

What's your favorite part of what you do?

I live my dream. Every day is a blessing. I work with amazingly talented people exceeding expectations. I achieve things every day. I love the challenge of what I do.

There are two types of people in the world, those that wonder what happened and those who make things happen.

Shane Weger

Experienced chef.

SHANE WEGER

How does a positive attitude contribute to what you do?

You definitely have to have a positive attitude with a career in hospitality, especially with your kitchen team and your waiting staff. The better your attitude is, the further you will go in your career in this industry.

A negative attitude reflects on how you work and what you do. When you are having an off-day, this reflects in your food. You have to have a positive attitude, even when you are having a bad day.

When did you learn that?

This is something I learned from working with people, through watching their body language. It's a key point for a good working environment.

Positive people are more willing to help you with everything. This rubs off on you and makes your life easier in the transition going from apprentice to becoming a qualified chef. And, a positive attitude makes a good impression on the people you are teaching.

Did you ever experience a personal defeat?

I had a personal defeat with a function that I did as a fourth-year apprentice. I was left on my own to do a wedding for 150 people. I accidentally grabbed the wrong tray of steaks and served them raw instead of medium rare! When you have to start again, you learn fast. I was disappointed with myself and there were repercussions from that. I'm human and I make mistakes, but I make sure this doesn't happen again.

Have you ever had to deal with old-school mentality?

I worked with an old head chef who had been in the industry for a long time. He was very set in his ways. The best way to deal with him was to ignore him and continue with working, which made life easier at that time.

Does your kitchen environment offer flexibility for working parents?

I am a father and need specific days off work each week for child care. Our roster is flexible, which allows for birthdays, sick days time off. In this day and age, the kitchen has to be flexible for parents.

Being a small country town we give both men and women opportunities and the women put in the hard work as much as the men do.

What keeps you motivated on a daily basis?

There is always going to be challenges when you walk into the kitchen, not knowing what the day will bring. You look at what produce you have, which keeps you motivated and looking for different ideas, check out at what other places are offering. You have to have passion in what you do, keep yourself motivated and keep your ideas open.

What do you consider to be your weaknesses?

That would come down to what dishes I am cooking especially living in a country town. I have never been into the fine dining. My weakness with my cooking skills is my limitation in cooking Middle Eastern and Asian dishes.

This is such a widespread community of chefs. We get together and brainstorm what we can do and what we are good at. What we can't do we ask each other. We work together getting different ideas and inspiration from each other.

What are common mistakes people make achieving success?

Failure would be the biggest one. A lot of chefs come in, thinking they know it all. When they fail, they can't actually handle criticism.

How do you inspire others?

By being a strong leader and being able to teach to a cook, a chef or an apprentice on how to communicate, approach others and train them at any level. You cannot talk down to your staff as your staff is part of the team. You always have to have a positive attitude. You have to know that they are on your side and everyone is on the same level.

Who has inspired you the most?

Two of my TAFE lecturers. One got me to work at a banquet for 600 people. This set me on the path to my career in cooking. The other was a head chef I worked with. She leads by example and inspired me because of her temperament. I want everyone in my team to know that I have a good temperament.

What's your vision for the future?

I would really love to own a little café. A family run business where I can create and do all that I want to do. This is one of my dreams, to work for myself in my own establishment.

You're only as good as the last dish that you send out.

Stephen Lunn

Stephen Lunn trained with the Sheraton Group in Western Australia and throughout Australia and the UK. Was teaching Certificate I and II in Hospitality, RSA and Barista courses. As a VET Teacher, he won 'Tasmania Trainer of the Year Awards' in 2011 and 2015. And, the 2015 Australian VET teacher/Trainer of the Year and Western Australia's 'Most Outstanding Chef' in 1999. He won a Gold Award at the 'Ireland International Salon Culinaire' and at National and State levels. He is State President of the Tasmanian Chapter of the Australian Culinary Federation, which involves competitions and education for chefs, cooks, apprentices, and culinary students.

STEPHEN LUNN

What is the most challenging part of your work?

What I find difficult, in this day and age, is the attitude people have; not only young people but the older generation too. It seems that it's the young people's fault, which isn't true. The older generation has to understand that the young people learn differently and want different things and we have to adjust to that. And the younger generation needs to take responsibility for their own actions and not rely on others.

Tell me about a difficult situation and how you handled it?

A difficult situation can be anything. It may be a complaint about what you cook. You can either take it to heart and be insulted, or you can learn from this and give the customer what they want. Or it may be a situation where you have to fire somebody and some don't take very kindly to this. You learn along the way.

Please share about your teaching career?

When I was training apprentices who were straight out of school, they didn't have the skills or the qualifications to continue. An opportunity came up for me to teach at the secondary school level. This program is now the first port of call for the industry in Tasmania, which I have developed over the past ten years. I just finished teaching with Year 11 and Year 12 students and I am very proud of this program Certificate II – Kitchen Operations.

Now I am looking for a new challenge. Whether that be going back into the kitchen, working with apprentices or with the government in the hospitality industry.

How do you instill the right mindset for your students?

You have to lead by example. Students see that I am enthused by what I teach. I run my own cooking school and catering business and I have a little vineyard and small truffière. I am very hands-on working in different places and at functions. Students see what I teach and do.

When you are enthusiastic about what you do, you take them on this journey and it's not hard to engage them in this way. I don't understand other teachers saying it is difficult to engage their students. I think if you show interest in what you teach, students learn. They all want to learn and hear that we're doing the right thing.

You spoke about being transient and changing jobs. Can you please elaborate on this?

This is something that chefs do. Certainly, after qualifying, you go overseas and spend some time eating their food and experiencing different cultures. It is something to do, however, not everyone will do this. We have plenty of international chefs coming to Australia, so we get the exposure anyway. Being transient gives you experience in many kitchens, employing different nationalities.

For your own personal growth, find out where produce comes from as this is an important part of our trade.

What's your vision for the future?

To bring the training package into a modern sense, as this will help young people to think this as a lifetime career. Everybody wants everything now. If they are still there in two years time, they feel they have been there forever. I want to see the right people coming in, as this is a highly skilled industry.

How are you putting this into place?

I am working with the Australian Government at a national level. The Australian Culinary Federation solely represents cooks and chefs. Chefs are ready to change. The whole industry is ready for change and we have to go about making sure we get that change right. This is going to be a hard sell for 'old-school' chefs.

We need good chefs committed to a professional trade. As chefs, we were always told that we have an unsociable trade. Every trade is now unsociable (and I don't really like saying that because you become Very Social within your own space). The world is such a 24/7 operation that people can't use that against us anymore as a negative. They have to stop saying that about our industry. I used to love doing split shifts. I went to the gym. I went to the pub to have a pint, or have a little power nap; I love the whole romance of this industry.

Why do you love to cook?

Because I love to eat, so I am satisfying my own personal wants. The more I got into cooking, the more people enjoyed what I did. I enjoy cooking for people to make their day and to put a smile on their face. When you cook for your kids, your family or your friends, they get a chance to relax without cooking themselves and that's a good thing.

My heritage is Dutch, but I did not grow up with this. I picked my food influences and likes from wherever I traveled and I know what I like to eat. I remember being on the Greek Islands and every day I went down to the docks to get local vegetables from the growers to cook. It is more than a source of fuel, it's a labor of love.

Ask a lot of questions and question all the time. Expect nothing and work hard. Success will come.

Stephen Shadbolt

Executive Chef Colonial Tramcar Restaurant

STEPHEN SHADBOLT

Why did you become a chef?

I started getting involved as a student cooking at home. Then over a period of time, I got interested and experimented with recipes. From there I decided to look for an apprenticeship in cooking. I started when I was 18. I had just left school and was pretty lucky to get a job.

During my apprenticeship, I worked in a French restaurant for three years and then I worked in fine dining restaurants. I am good at being creative and one of the things I love is being part of the kitchen. This is a natural thing that I do really well.

What are your favorite skills in cooking?

I am pretty much an all-rounder when it comes to cooking. Knife skills are always something you can stick with. Always use fresh produce with menu development, when trying new recipes and changing the menu regularly. We have to adapt to new things all the time, as food trends are always changing.

What daily challenges do you face?

There are numerous challenges that I have to face. Working with the staff I have to be a counselor, a motivator, a mentor and a trainer; and I have to consistently produce high-quality standards for the diner. A major focus is training and mentoring apprentices, with a skill base that will carry them through the whole of their careers and beyond.

I have to constantly source high-quality ingredients from week to week while working within budget guidelines. I have to do justice with this produce while having respect for the ingredients that I work with. I have to be well prepped and organized, working within time constraints during Colonial Tramcar Restaurant service.

I have to maintain a respectful and creative working environment and be able to cater for all dietary requirements. It's not just the vegetarians anymore, as now it's celiac, fructose intolerance, dairy-free, and vegans.

Then there is keeping your work and life balance on an even keel, especially with a family.

If you were given 1000 acres tax-free land, what would it be like and what would you do with this?

Something with great views, preferably near the ocean with nice surroundings and definitely with sustainability.

Have you practiced organic farming at all?

No, I haven't as I have not had the time for that yet. It would be great to know how to do this, as this is what people want these days and that's good for everyone.

What sort of atmosphere do you have in the kitchen?

One where everyone works together well and everyone respects each other. We have a lot of fun as well as we all work toward the same goal. My staff has worked with me for a few years now and even when staff leave, they still keep in contact. We currently have 20 staff, working a seven day per week operation.

Chefs do come and go. With our working environment here, we are pretty stable. Some people like to work in different restaurants and to have the latest restaurants on their CVs.

The Colonial Tramcar Restaurant is a production kitchen. Some people miss having the adrenaline rush during service, whereas we don't do service from the kitchen directly. We produce restaurant quality meals which are then cooked on the trams. To create restaurant quality meals of choice, such as how you want a steak cooked. We produce larger volumes using cook-chill, seal the meat and the vegetables and then blast chill them.

We would classify our meals as first-class airline food. We produce around 400 meals a day and sometimes more. This is a lot of production for 365 days a year.

With your days off what do you enjoy doing the most?

Actually, I eat out at restaurants and spend time with family. I do gardening and catch up on things at home. My wife is a chef, so she does some of the cooking; so that works out well.

What was the best business advice that you've been given?

Restaurants are not so easy and can be hard to make a go of. You have to keep on top of everything; know everything that is going on; and know where you can keep the costs down.

What is something special about being a chef?

You have to passionately want to be a chef. You can't do this for the sake of doing it if you want to do it properly. You have to be enthusiastic and you have to want to get up every day to be in the kitchen, work with fresh produce and be creative. It can't be just a job, for the sake of doing a job. You have to really want to do this.

If you enjoy what you do, you'll never work another day in your life. ~ **Confucius**

Terase Davidson

Founder and Chef of 'Taste Byron Bay' – Catering, Private Dining, Events, Food Tours and Cooking Classes.

TERASE DAVIDSON

Why do you wear a chef's apron?

Unknown to me the 'seed' for me to become a chef was firmly planted as a young girl.

I grew up in a family of seven chefs and I spent many a family holiday as a young girl, standing on milk crates in my aunty and uncle's Byron Bay 'The Fig Tree Restaurant', asking my uncle Charly a million and one questions.

In my early 20's, I packed my bags and headed to London and soon I found myself working in the fast-paced finance industry managing events across the globe. And although I loved my job in London, I had this increasingly overwhelming desire to follow my heart and create a career in food.

At the age of 33, I came home to Australia to do my Commercial Cooking Certificate III and rather brazenly walked into one of Sydney's top fine dining restaurants, 'Aqua Dining' at Milson's Point and asked for a job! With no real restaurant experience, just simply armed with an abundance of enthusiasm and an insatiable appetite to learn and grow my knowledge base. Head Chef Jeff Turnbull said "Yes," and I started the very next day! I worked myself harder than I ever thought possible with 26 hours at TAFE per week and around 70 hours in the kitchen honing my art. And lucky for me, I was quickly rewarded for my ambition, ability, and eagerness to learn on the move, with a promotion to Chef De Partie within three months of starting my new career.

After five years of crazy hours in the kitchen, my body told me loud and clear that this was not going to be sustainable long term. So, I headed back to London and into the corporate world to give my body a rest. However, I had this constant inner voice on my shoulder saying "Were you really put on this earth to not follow your dream Terase?" So with increasing urgency and focus, I set about working out a way that I could combine my skills and passion as a chef, together with my knowledge and expertise in event management and 'Taste Byron Bay' was born!

Is there a food that is out of favor?

For me, the best and biggest shift in recent years is that more and more people are moving away from heavily processed foods and simply getting back to basics. Which I think can only be a good thing for our minds, bodies and the environment. Not only is this shift back to basics good for our diets, but it's also super important for meaningful social interaction and the strengthening of the family tapestry. There is so much joy and happiness that can be gained by the simple act of sharing a meal with loved ones and talking about the day, giving children in particular a chance to talk about anything that might be troubling them and help them navigate their way through the often challenging world of social media and online bullying.

How do you make your business sustainable?

I guess sustainability can mean many things to many people, but for me initially starting my own business from scratch, sustainability literally meant often just keeping my head above water in the beginning.

Once I got over the shock of throwing myself in at the deep end and the steep learning curve that followed. I had a chance, for example, to look at the business and how we manage waste in the kitchen and we now proudly donate surplus food to our local 'Food Research Bank' which supports local homeless people and folks doing it tough.

Have you ever been down a rabbit hole?

"Oh yes, the dreaded rabbit hole." I've been down there for sure! I left a really good job in Sydney to follow this little food dream of mine. The first 18 months were way harder than I'd ever anticipated. I've definitely learned that I am way more resilient than I'd ever given myself credit for. And that often the key to success in business is your ability to regularly access your business, through the neutral eyes of a third party, taking out all the emotion and making the necessary adjustments to your business plan and taking that change in direction when you need to. Ah and wholeheartedly accepting that running your own business is not easy, because if it was easy, then everyone would be doing it!

What's your vision for the future?

To continue to inspire people to believe they deserve good food with flavor, to change the way people shop and for everyone to live with more sustainability. To be at one with the rhythm of the seasons and with the abundance of local produce that we become appreciative for our health and the economy.

I firmly believe, that with a little bit of forward planning, it's relatively easy to shift the way in which we shop and live. Because we all deserve food with flavor! We've just got to go out there and get it!

What does food symbolize?

For me, I think food has an amazing ability to take us on a journey, to recall happy times with family and friends or a dreamy holiday and can often provide comfort and warmth during challenging times. Really, when you think about it, whenever we celebrate a big occasion like a birthday, getting a new job, going on a date with a special someone, finishing a big exam or the birth of a child, more often than not we say

"Let's go out to dinner to celebrate." So for me, yeah I guess, food has always been about celebrating food with family and friends. It doesn't have to be super food fancy, it really is just the simple act of sharing food with family and friends around the table. That means the most to me.

I've always been fascinated by food's ability to bring people together.

Vic Cherikoff

Author, scientist and entrepreneur with a focus on Australian wild foods and medicines. He has written a number of peer-reviewed scientific papers, six books on wild food and promotes Australian resources for better nutrition and health.

VIC CHERIKOFF

What are your success habits?

Persistence is probably the main one. This is because of the unique niche which I used for my culinary adventures. I am a scientist by training and a pioneer in the wild food industry. I was lucky in that I had these amazing flavors at my disposal and I thought if I could introduce these unique flavors to a few chefs and supply their food outlets then we could have an authentic Australian cuisine. I thought it would be an overnight success, as chefs could use wild foods and their own creativity to promote themselves and Australia as a food destination.

However, what I realized is that many chefs are taught cuisine styles rather than taking the flavor of ingredients as the primary keys to unlocking great meals. We still learn to cook with ingredients, because of established cuisine. Concepts can be mixed up as with fusion cuisine, but the components still reflect recognized food traditions. Unfortunately, when brand new flavors are presented, most chefs are not trained to create dishes using the building blocks of taste.

I spent decades using my background in biochemistry, anatomy, and physiology to take a different approach and worked to explain the dozen or so tastes that we can detect in foods and how to combine, balance and enhance ingredients using this empirical method. I am not a trained chef, but with courses, demonstrations, writing curricula, blogs, a website, and my own books, I presented chefs my ideas on how to use wild foods just by going by their taste.

I also ran Australian food promotions all over the world in five-star hotels, tourist resorts, on six-star cruise ships, railways, airlines and the list goes on. In fact, I could change what I do day to day and travel the world featuring my version of Australian food culture because globally, more people than ever before are open-minded when it comes to new taste experiences.

But back to the flavors in foods: The challenge I faced was to define the wild ingredients I had available in terms of their nature as we perceive them physiologically. There are thirteen taste/smell groups in food – twelve important ones. The thirteenth of these flavors is astringency, which is not a flavor that we typically want in a dish, but which can appear in unripe fruits example: Illawarra plums. The addition of lemon juice effectively masks astringency.

If a chef understands food flavors and knows how flavors are paired to complement or mask another, then it is possible to create a winning dish every time. I often use the example of the Caesar salad which has all the core 12 flavors in a well-made recipe and is undoubted, the most popular dish in Caucasian eateries all over the world. It also contains the textural variation that helps contribute to its popularity.

This educational process has taken three and a half decades. But we now finally see Australian cuisine based around wild foods, as all the go now and even a few foraging chefs.

Another angle that I am embracing now is the nutritional one. Wild foods are perfect to top up our nutritional status as they are very good sources of micronutrients. These are limiting in modern foods and include antioxidants, anti-inflammatories, anti-allergens, good sugars, functional organic acids, bioavailable minerals and a whole lot more. This is being taken up by spa resorts, aged care facilities and other food outlets with a health focus, but also goes directly to consumers as wild foods appear to address many of the symptoms of the diseases of nutrition.

How have you found success?

My passion was for the wild food and medicinal resources of Australia, their flavors and functionality. I invested time, effort and all the money I had, could borrow or get through cash flow and worked flat out for years. I used to say "Bite off more than you can chew and then chew like hell." But looking back I would have preferred to work smarter, not harder.

I cajoled chefs, inviting them to use the many ingredients I could source myself and through Aboriginal communities. I ran the courses, wrote the books, garnered promotional support, in my own PR program and even funded, produced and promoted a 13-part television series called 'Dining Downunder' which aired in 48 countries and coincided with my international Australian food promotions.

I essentially built a lifestyle business, but one which I thoroughly enjoyed and it never seemed like work. What I learned though, was that it is better not to have to educate your market. Find a hungry crowd and solve their most pressing problem.

Sometimes what you think will work, takes off. Other times it frustratingly doesn't.

My wild food super-nutritional product is making serious inroads and provides amazing health benefits to anyone who eats. On the other hand, I developed an award-winning, natural antimicrobial (a sanitizer for foods and other related ingredients, even packaging). I thought that since it cut food waste, enhanced food safety and replaced synthetic chemical preservatives in many applications it would be a huge success. However, it has taken over five years to gain momentum (and this mainly in the USA) while the food industry here still sprouts empty words about food waste and safety. In the words of Ned Kelly: "Such is life."

In summary, my philosophy is that as you live your days as you live your life.

If you love what you do and it pays the bills then you'll have a life well lived. I feel that as a pioneer of the wild food industry I am also leaving a legacy that others can take over and make work for themselves.

Authors
Final Word

AUTHORS FINAL WORD

I trust that these stories have motivated you to pursue a career in hospitality.

The key to progress is work. Ask "What would you like to accomplish?" Continuously buckle down and go the extra mile with the end goal to success. Let your fervent love of cooking become your joy. Continue celebrating and extending the various delights of life that encompass you.

Self-exploration can be a powerful way to become acquainted with who you truly are. Challenge, or better still shed, false convictions and beliefs you have acquired about yourself and get clear about what you really need for your life. In doing so you will learn, develop and feel you're a piece of something significant that is bigger than yourself. There you will find your success.

Share your creativity with the world! Make your failures your best friend. You need to be passionately inspired and keep that twinkle in your eyes.

Cooking with love gives nourishment to the soul. Ignite the spark with your working career. You can if you Believe you can!

ABOUT THE AUTHOR

Juliana is an author, entrepreneur, and healer.

Born and raised in Melbourne, Juliana is a mother of two sons and has been married for more than 48 years. For 17 of those years, Juliana and her husband Tony operated a large biodynamic dairy farm where various healing modalities were used on the land and on the animals. Juliana loved her work with the cows and calves and pioneered complementary medicine to treat cows (and humans) with Reiki, Kinesiology, Massage, Homeopathy and Living Threads frequencies. She went on to work with Alex Podolinsky, a student of Rudolf Steiner, to commercialize biodynamic milk in Australia.

Juliana's passion for knowledge about color thread frequencies led her to study in New Zealand with Les Elphick. He handpicked her to be the only person to share his coveted information with. She went on to print a catalog of 2400 black and white color frequencies for Kinesiologists. At the request of Cam Dawson, she produced a color version of the catalog that was sold worldwide.

Her first publishing success was the book *Colour Cotton Therapy*. She sold 2000 copies in the first three months. Her next publishing efforts were the *GenHarmony* metaphysical cards, followed by the *Living Threads* book featuring almost 5000 frequencies. Since then, she has created nine *Living Threads* online healing courses, including 41 videos. These have been recognized throughout Australia, New Zealand, the United Kingdom, the United States, South Africa, and Europe.

Juliana's most recent publishing triumph is the *Romancing the Rose* – an eleven-book series. The series of beautifully presented picture books feature pages where each rose conveys a different message. With these books, Juliana invites the reader to be transported to a sentimental place and time to experience sheer enjoyment beyond the sorrows and cares of the world.

Her professional associations include the International Institute of Complementary Therapists and AON Practitioner Insurance. She has traveled and worked throughout Australia, India, Nepal, Vanuatu, New Zealand, Singapore, Tonga, Ghana, Ireland, Poland, and Brazil.

Juliana Frances is the author of *Chefs Stories Unmasked* and lives in New South Wales Australia with her husband.

www.JulianaFrances.com

Recommended
Resources

IN THIS BOOT CAMP YOU WILL DISCOVER...

> A whole mind-body integration in an understandable and productive way

> How to create total freedom designed to eliminate old patterns of resistance

> How to expand your heart and mind towards achieving healthier relationships

> How to raise your vitality and love for cooking in a positive and insightful way

> Essential tips to navigate and implement your focus and direction in life

> How to breathe and take in all of life to boost your confidence and success

> How to get anything you desire and access total abundance, joy, and happiness

> Unique sources of information that will open new doorways to an exciting future

Create a sense of comradery with your fellow team members with this positive eye-opening source of information. There are no limitations to the rewards that you will achieve when you choose to invest time and energy in yourself.

Abundance, Health and Wellness, Relationships, and Addictions and are some of the topics of inner mastery discovered at these Boot Camps.

A wellspring of knowledge taught with a great sense of support offers variety and fun.

For more information

go to www.JulianaFrances.com

RECOMMENDED RESOURCES

For over 55 years Lifeline has been supporting Australian's in their time of need, receiving up to one million contacts for help a year.

If you or someone you know is in crisis, please call Lifeline 24/7 on 13 11 14 or visit www.lifeline.org.au

5% of the profits of this book will be donated to Lifeline, as I believe this service is essential to keep our people safe.